Success With The Media

Everything You Need To Survive Reporters And Your Organization

By Leonard Adam Sipes, Jr.

Leonard A. Sipes, LLC

Copyright © 2016, Leonard A. Sipes, Jr.

All rights reserved. Except for brief quotations cited in critical reviews or other articles, no part of this book may be used or reproduced in any manner without the written permission of the author.

No part of this publication may be reproduced, stored in a retrieval system, or transmitted, in any form or by any means, electronic, mechanical, photocopying, recording, or otherwise without written permission of the author.

The author's email address is leonardsipes@gmail.com.

Printed by CreateSpace Publishing, North Charleston, SC

Printed in the United States of America

ACKNOWLEDGEMENTS

Spokespeople cannot survive media encounters without the support of their agency heads. I have been fortunate to work for news savvy executives who understand the value of good media and public relations. The presence of these men and women and their support during times of immense stress is the principal reason I have survived some of the toughest public affairs assignments possible. I'm appreciative that there are seasoned professionals who understand the "dance" that occurs with every media contact.

I would also like to thank my wife Concetta and my two children, Cynthia and Kelly. Their love and that of God's has given me the strength to continue in this very strange profession for as long as I have.

Advance Editorial edited this book at http://www.advancededitorial.com. I am grateful for their guidance.

Use of Names

The names used in this book are fictitious unless otherwise noted.

Use of Incidents

The use of incidents and examples in this book are based on 35 years of talking to the media while representing four national and state agencies. They are also based on hundreds of conversations with reporters and peers in the public and private sectors. Unless noted, incidents cited do not represent specific people or organizations.

Forthcoming Books

"Emergency Media in the Digital Age"

"Media Relations and Criminal Justice"

Contact Information

Contact me at leonardsipes@gmail.com or via http://leonardsipes.com

TABLE OF CONTENTS

INTRODUCTION..21

CHAPTER ONE: THESE ARE DANGEROUS TIMES..33

CHAPTER TWO: YOUR RELATIONSHIP WITH THE MEDIA..69

CHAPTER THREE: THE ART OF THE INTERVIEW..93

CHAPTER FOUR: BREAKING BAD NEWS FIRST..189

CHAPTER FIVE: THE CARE AND FEEDING OF SPOKESPEOPLE...235

CHAPTER SIX: THE HIRING PROCESS: DO WE LIE TO PROSPECTIVE CANDIDATES?........................257

CHAPTER SEVEN: BUILDING RELATIONSHIPS: MARKETING...271

CHAPTER EIGHT: MEDIA YOU CONTROL: WEBSITES, PODCASTS AND SOCIAL MEDIA...............................323

CONTACT INFORMATION......................................353

QUOTES

"Nothing can now be believed which is seen in a newspaper. Truth itself becomes suspicious being put in that polluted vehicle. I have almost ceased to read the newspapers."

—Thomas Jefferson

"Public opinion is everything. With public sentiment nothing can fail; without it, nothing can succeed. Consequently, he who molds public opinion goes deeper than he who enacts statutes and pronounces decisions. Our government rests on public opinion."

—Abraham Lincoln

"As a young reporter at The Sun in the 1950's, Somerville was told by the news desk to go to City Hall and asked the mayor to react to something the mayor clearly didn't want to talk about. "Timidly, the cub reporter approached the mayor and stated: 'Mr. Mayor, my desk has asked me to ask you…' "The mayor put his ear to his own desk, muttered, and said, 'Mr. Somerville, my desk tells me to tell your desk to go [bleep] itself.'"

—Baltimore Sun, "Perspective," 9-2-2001

"I believe in the profession of journalism. I believe that the public journal is a public trust; that all connected with it are, to the full measure of their responsibility, trustees for the public; that acceptance of lesser service than the public service is a betrayal of this trust."

—Walter Williams, "The Journalist's Creed," 1914

"Sipes, I'm sick and tired of you bureaucrats who can't answer a straight question. I don't see how the hell you all can live with yourselves. Bureaucrats, bureaucrats, bureaucrats! The whole [bleeping] world is filled with bureaucrats!"

—The Baltimore Sun Re-write Desk. 1989

"You reporters should have printed what he meant, not what he said."

—Earl Bush, press aide to Richard Daley.

"I believe in equality for everyone, except reporters and photographers."

—Gandhi

"Whoever controls the media—the images—controls the culture."

—Allen Ginsburg

"Journalism is merely history's first draft."

—Geoffrey C. Ward

"The newspapers, especially those in the East, are amazingly superficial… and all large number of news gatherers are either cynics at heart or following the orders and policies of the owners of their papers."

—Franklin D. Roosevelt

"I read in the newspapers that they are going to have 30 minutes of intellectual stuff on television every Monday from 7:30 to 8...to educate America. They couldn't educate America if they started at 6:30."

—Groucho Marx

"Do not read the newspapers."

—Henry David Thoreau

"My doctors told me this morning my blood pressure is down so low that I can start reading the newspapers."

—Ronald Reagan

"Everything is being compressed into tiny tablets. You take a little pill of news every day—23 minutes—and that's supposed to be enough."

—Walter Cronkite

ACCOLADES FOR "SUCCESS WITH THE MEDIA"

John Verrico

"This is a must-have book for people entering the media relations profession, as well as for the veteran public information officer. Sipes' insight serves as a smack-in-the-face reminder of what can go right or wrong in the interactions between public organizations and the media. Sage advice and great examples throughout!"

John Verrico is the President of the National Association of Government Communicators at http://www.nagc.com/.

Kathleen Kennedy Townsend

Len Sipes was a great guide and mentor to me when I was Lt. Governor. Now he has brought his many years of wit, wisdom and fabulous stories to inspire a new generation of public relation professionals. He shows the winning qualities are curiosity, dedication to the truth and building trust not only with the press but also within one's own agency...which at times can be even more difficult!!!

Kathleen Kennedy Townsend is an adjunct professor at the Georgetown Public Policy Institute, a visiting fellow at the Kennedy School of Government at Harvard University, and senior Nitze fellow at St. Mary's College of Maryland. She is on the board of directors of the John F. Kennedy Library Foundation plus many others.

Donna Ledbetter

Sipes offers great insights, and many of the questions the book answers are exactly the sort of advice I would have asked for to assist me in starting my own public affairs career. The writing is honest, easy to understand, and gripping at some points. The pacing and vivid imagery helped me connect with the lessons offered. It's a good book and I believe that thousands of others will agree.

Donna Ledbetter is CEO of Advanced Editorial at www.advancededitorial.com.

Kitty Wooley

If I were going into a media relations job for the first time, I would drop everything and read Len Sipes's book from cover to cover. Len has written the book he wishes he'd had early in his career. His intention to leave a legacy for his successors in the field, and to convey the value of navigating an increasingly complex task with integrity under all sorts of conditions, succeeds.

Because Len pulls no punches, this distillation of his experience will be upsetting to some and a sought-after resource for others, particularly young employees who are moving into this kind of work in federal agency communications shops. Much can be learned about the entire ecosystem in which this kind of work occurs, and about how to gain confidence, how to earn the trust of senior leaders and reporters, how to work with deadlines, and how to handle the occasional, unavoidable, crash related to inaccurate information.

The book contains three sentences that will be recognized by most every senior employee who works in a large bureaucracy: "I was astounded as to how difficult it was to find answers within the bureaucracy. Everyone knew of someone else who was more qualified than themselves to provide the right information. I was also equally dismayed at times by the misinformation provided."

Len describes at length the role and importance of each competency he deems necessary for a career in media relations. The book reflects the personal price exacted from Len because he chose to break that new ground in addition to standing between worlds whose mission and operational speed differ greatly. And, in my opinion, that honesty is one of the best things about the book.

Kitty Wooley is the founder of Senior Fellows and Friends at http://seniorfellowsandfriends.blogspot.com/ designed to foster innovation and change within federal agencies and beyond. Kitty administered the US Department of Education's internal innovation platform. Kitty's website is http://www.energizingconnection.com/. Her LinkedIn site is https://www.linkedin.com/in/kitty.

Robert Weinhold

Len captures the gritty, ground level media relations insights and tactics needed to survive in today's fast paced worldwide thirst for information environment. A great resource for both newly challenged and experienced practitioners, Len's body of knowledge is not only evident, it's there for the taking. I'd highly recommend this publication as a must have tool for surviving the game, a game which could end your career as quickly as it began.

Rob Weinhold is Principal of Fallston Group, a Baltimore based crisis management and communications firm, see http://www.fallstongroup.com/.

J. Scott Whitney

When things go SOUTH in public safety, the first face the media sees may well be the Public Information Officer. The outcomes of the crisis du jour being redemption or riots may turn on the quality of this encounter. Mr. Sipes speaks from his experience in the trenches about the importance of creating and nurturing the relationships of management and media and some of the consequences of failure. These are his stories.

J. Scott Whitney, works for a federal government agency and was a captain (retired) with the Maryland State Police.

INTRODUCTION

The Author

I have 35 years of media relations experience. As I finish this book, I am the Senior Public Affairs Specialist and Social Media Manager for a federal agency in Washington, D.C. I have personally handled thousands of media inquiries and administrated the response to thousands more. I have been a spokesperson for well-known, national causes. I traveled the country speaking at conferences on media relations and proactive efforts. I advised presidential and political campaigns, well-known national agencies and assisted scores of organizations seeking assistance.

I have a wide array of national and local awards, including best customer service, best use of technology, and top awards for podcasting, audio and television hosting, and production. I created the first radio and television podcast series in both state and federal governments. I rose steadily in rank and pay for my media and promotional work. As I write this section, I am about to receive my seventh media relations award this year.

Who Is This Book For?

I wrote this book for spokespeople and individuals likely to talk to reporters. It's also for executives who make most media decisions. Lastly, I believe journalists and news management will find an insider's account of bureaucracies and their response to media inquiries interesting and insightful.

Why Read This Book?

What will this book do for you? Success with the Media addresses the needs of new and veteran spokespersons. It provides the stories, tips, and insight to succeed in this vastly misunderstood profession. It breaks new ground. It discusses an endless array of issues not covered by other books.

If you understand the media relations and organizational process, you will prosper. If not, you and your organization could face a very public demise.

Do you know that some of your top executives may talk to the media without telling you? Have you ever had an agency head tell you something that wasn't true that ended up on the front page of the morning newspaper? Have you ever been given advice by a technical expert that turned out to be wrong, and you had to retract the statement? These are all real examples of life in the media relations trenches. You need to know that these pitfalls exist and you need to recognize what you can do to avoid them.

You need knowledge of social and digital media; you need it summarized for quick lessons and information as to what works and what doesn't. You need to understand how to market and promote your organization, how to break bad news and how to take care of yourself and those around you.

Knowing what to do will earn the respect of your executives. I have never lost an agency head due to negative publicity; their gratitude provided me with both job security and an endless series of promotions and pay increases. You will become an invaluable part of your organization. You will gain prestige; staff at all levels will seek your opinions.

The book also provides management with the knowledge to properly guide their spokespersons. They will understand what happens and why. It allows them to become a team leader and use the capacities of their public affairs team effectively.

Finally, reporters and news executives will have a better understanding of what happens when they call for information or comment. If they know the cumbersome internal processing of media inquiries, they will understand that confusion and delay is often an inevitable part of the process. Imprecise reactions may not carry the negative inferences many reporters impose on sloppy or inaccurate replies.

Success with the Media examines a process that ranges far beyond simply talking to reporters. It reviews the internal and external means of responding to requests from news operations. It's a series of actions far more complicated than many of us think and is almost untouched by other books. It's the guidance I looked for early in my career.

Success with the Media is not a basic primer on media relations. There are many elementary materials. The book is based on my 14 years representing Maryland's largest agency and 21 years as an information manager and spokesperson for two federal clearinghouses and one agency. Most of the book focuses on my experience as the Director of Public Information for the Maryland Department of Public Safety and Correctional Services where I did 90 percent of my media interviews. You will see shortened references to the "Department of Public Safety" or simply "the Department" throughout.

The book describes a sometimes harsh reality of multiple exchanges between spokespeople, bureaucrats, and reporters. The stories are based on real events and much of the book was written as I experienced them. It's a probing examination of what happens when a reporter contacts any bureaucracy. It's not just a series of stories; it includes tips and observations to help spokespeople survive and thrive. It strips the varnish off process and provides a long-overdue examination of the news interview in a wide variety of formats.

I take everyone to task, from reporters to bureaucrats to spokespeople. What I want the book to do is start a conversation at all levels to improve the provision of information to the public. My guess is that my many friends in the media and public affairs will, at times, find the discussion uncomfortable. But as I stated, my observations are based on real events and conversations with hundreds of people in public affairs and news organizations. I make no apology for my observations.

Combat Public Relations

My early choice for a title for this book was "Combat Public Relations." It refers to a conversation I had with public affairs officers in Boulder, Colorado, while I was attending a training course in public relations sponsored by the U.S. Department of Justice. Some were new at the job while others had many years of experience. We had drifted into conversation after the evening meal. The discussion, quite naturally, focused on our jobs.

"I want combat pay," said a spokesperson for a large government agency. Experienced spokespeople around the table quickly agreed.

"The trolls I deal with in my agency drive me crazy. The media are a pain, but I understand them," he said. "What I have a hard time accepting is the screwy nature of my own bureaucracy."

Veteran spokespeople believed that their agencies were often impediments to good media relations. We were suspicious of the media and aware of reporters with questionable ethics, but we were often more apprehensive of our own people. The consensus was that, if we were left alone, the job would be much more agreeable. Unfettered, we could do a better job of protecting our agencies.

We understood that news people and their organizations could be dangerous, but there was a cadence, a timing, a personality to most reporters and their bureaucracies that you could understand. At times, we were more comfortable with them than with our own agencies.

Hundreds of Conversations

Throughout the years I have had hundreds of conversations with people who speak for business, government, and associations. Hundreds more were held with reporters. These interactions are the foundation of this book. Through these exchanges, I found more agreement than disagreement regarding the fundamentals of our jobs.

It was interesting to hear veteran spokespeople for large corporations, the military, universities, nonprofits, and government voice similar opinions.

I was told that the way to control negative media was to get out in front of it by releasing tough news first. They said that the majority of news people were decent and the stereotype of the unscrupulous reporter (while true) was overblown. Others advised me that my own organization would probably be the source of my greatest difficulties, and that interactions with the media could be mild in comparison. Some told me that my reputation with the media would count as much as or more than the details offered during interviews.

Laced throughout the conversations was one central theme—that ours is an immensely complex and interesting job that is often learned through trial and error. They were correct. There are few advanced books on interview techniques and none dealing with the complexities of the organizations we work for. There are a wide array of books and materials on public relations, but few (if any) seem to be grounded in our reality.

Existing materials warned me not to go "off the record" in conversations with reporters. Veteran spokespersons told me that they did it all the time. Other documents provided extensive instruction on setting up a press conference. Seasoned spokespersons warned me to use press conferences sparingly, if at all.

I watched with dismay as new spokespeople came to the job only to leave a short time later. Their primary complaint was that the job they were offered had little to do with realities of their position. Even news people making the jump to public relations found that they (and the people they worked for) misunderstood the realities of the job. News reporting is to public affairs as a professional baseball player is to coaching. Doing one does not mean you can do the other.

We May Disagree

I have made it my goal to listen to those who have done this job successfully. Their guidance has been, at times, both startling and hard to comprehend. But over time, I have found that they have been correct. This book is my attempt to pass on the accumulated knowledge.

You are more than welcome to disagree with my assertions. For example, I believe there are differences in the accountability required of public and private organizations. While I feel strongly that the government should be as open as possible, those representing corporations believe that their accountability lies more with their shareholders and customers. In that world, they believe reporters can be an enemy of open thought and discussion, a place where innovation and risk give way to media-designated winners and losers.

Some company and government representatives will issue a terse statement in response to media inquiries. Yet I believe that some within the media see written statements as indications that an organization may have something to hide. Yes, this is changing as more media inquiries are made through e-mail and text messages. In some cases, written statements are acceptable and even encouraged by media on deadline. But I still believe that conversations are the best method of responding to media inquiries.

It's obvious that we will agree to disagree on how to best represent our agencies. I still believe, however, that experienced spokespeople find common ground more often than not.

Media Relations Has Changed

Media relations have changed immensely in the last 10 years. The ranks of reporters have greatly declined, up to a third (or more) in many newsrooms. They have to do more with less, sometimes much less. Media deadlines have changed from preparing for the noon and 6:00 p.m. news to immediacy.

Our jobs have also dramatically changed. When I started, knowing media relations and being a good spokesperson was all that was required. We all did a bit of writing and promotions when we had time, but eighty percent of what we did was speak to reporters. Now we write extensively. We manage websites. We shoot and edit photos and video. We record our own radio programs. More inquiries than ever are conducted by e-mail and text messages. More than ever, reporters are relying on public affairs representatives to define stories. Social media and other sources of self-publishing have dramatically changed the landscape.

We are no longer solely dependent on the media to tell our stories, and that requires a wide array of new skills and ethics. For the media and organizational representatives, our jobs have never been more time consuming, tech-oriented, and stressful.

Misplaced Fear Of Reporters:

Surveys of trust in the media show endless declines and I understand why. According to a 2014 Gallup poll, "American's confidence in the media's ability to report the news fully, accurately and fairly has returned to an all-time low."

Cable news outlets are shouting matches and forums for the silliest observations. Ethical, unbiased and integrity-based reports can seem to be products of the past.

We (and people we work for) are somewhat horrified by what we see on television and hear on radio. What we read can be equally disconcerting. At times we seem to be incapable of having honest conversations with reporters and the public.

The inference some make that is that these are the characteristics of most reporters. That observation is a mistake.

The majority of reporters are just like us; they are looking to do the most effective job possible while minimizing difficulties. They are not looking to destroy you or your organization. They simply want to tell the truth. They can even become allies capable of more good than harm.

Too many media relations consultants and books play to the fear of the media to the point where it becomes dysfunctional and professionally dangerous. They are not the enemy. They can immensely evenhanded if your reputation for fairness precedes you.

Winning the War

The bottom-line advice of this book is an emphasis on winning the war, not the battle. Taking a long-range view of media relations dramatically increases the chance that your leadership and their mission will continue.

Those of us representing large, cumbersome agencies will find ourselves losing battles with the media. You cannot and should not expect to win every encounter. You can, however, prevail. You can gain the admiration and respect of media organizations and the public by employing the right strategies at the right time.

Building Relationships

The most important aspect of taking a long-range view is building relationships. We cannot succeed unless we build meaningful and productive interactions with the media and the public. Everything we are and all we can be must be built on trust. We must be seen as honorable people doing an honorable job. Anything short of that lofty goal spells disaster.

This book provides ideas and game plans to win battles and to build trust. I want your organization not only to survive, but thrive.

Resources

Resources and technologies come and go. What was relevant last year has often been replaced by new and more powerful platforms. Keeping up emerging strategies is a daunting task.

Please see my website at http://leonardsipes.com for recommended resources and organizations. There you will find an extensive list divided into four sections:

1. Daily Reading and Resources

2. Content Creation

3. Social Media

4. Emergency Media Management

What I Offer

I offer media and public relations services, consulting, speaking, social media, and recorded video and audio interviews (podcasting). If I can be of assistance, please contact me at leonardsipes@gmail.com, or my website, http://leonardsipes.com, or call toll free at 410-575-3127.

CHAPTER ONE: THESE ARE DANGEROUS TIMES

Stumbling into my house in Baltimore City, I was a dejected nine-year-old who had been in one of a series of fights with a boy who was larger and older. "Steve" was the neighborhood bully who seemed to take great delight in intimidating younger boys. I was tired of fighting back and constantly losing. That day, my father came to me, looked me over, saw the bruises and said, "You're going to have to figure out a way to beat him or find a way to finesse him."

"What?" was my defiant response.

"You can try to think of a way to beat him, but I don't think you can," he said. "You're going to have to figure out a way to live with him. You must rely on your intelligence and your ability to talk your way out of confrontations. It's either that, or constantly lose fights."

***

There are times when media relations is an ultimate challenge of diplomacy, tact, and skill. One of my principal concerns when I work with organizations is that many get it wrong. They make inappropriate media decisions during times of high stress, and they do it often. I am amazed when very caring, educated, and experienced senior managers make bad media decisions. The same holds true for some media relations professionals. So let's start with a discussion about who influences media decisions.

Who Influences Media Decisions?

People who decide what to say to the media have a wide variety of backgrounds. They range from senior executives to personnel and technical experts to attorneys, managers from the home office, and individuals designated to talk to the media. So when I say that many individuals who make media-related decisions get it wrong, I'm referring to everyone in the decision-making process. The larger the decision-making committee, the greater the potential for problems.

What is so important about the lines of communication? For some organizations, it means little. They do not have the burden of representing a policy or mission that is difficult or unpopular.

Their infrequent media requests are directed to day-to-day operations, and they often do not face immediate deadline pressures. They have the luxury of time and consultation with all concerned. For others, having established understandings about who makes media decisions under normal or difficult circumstances can be a lifesaver. For those who need the comfort of endless discussion and consensus of many stakeholders, God be with you.

The organizations I am addressing are the ones that simply do not have the time. Speed is not only necessary; it is crucial to their survival. To survive with speed, you have to have a plan. You have to know your organization, its data and its people. You have to be ready at a moment's notice.

Complexity of my Organizations

I was the Director of Public Information for the Maryland Department of Public Safety, a state law enforcement and correctional department, a $900 million, 12,000-employee operation encompassing 13 agencies and 8 boards and commissions, operating in over 100 locations throughout the state. The department focused mainly on correctional issues such as a variety of prison systems, as well as parole and community supervision issues plus law enforcement agencies. We supervised 150,000 criminal offenders and cases every day.

I worked with several full-time public information officers and a multitude of volunteer PIOs (public information officers). The volunteers had other full-time departmental jobs but occasionally spoke to the media.

We handled approximately 8,000 media "contacts" every year. The Washington D.C.-Baltimore, Maryland media market is one of the largest in the country and contained some of the most experienced and aggressive reporters.

At the time I began writing this book, I had been with the agency as director for 14 years, which was a record for state public information service. I did up to $4 million dollars a year in proactive marketing (per a regional advertising agency).

I previously served as a Senior Information Specialist and Director of Information Services for 10 years for two agencies in the Washington

D.C. area funded by the U.S. Department of Justice. As the current senior spokesperson and social media manager for a federal agency in Washington, D.C., I pioneered the use of radio and television shows (podcasts) and social media thus becoming a leader in proactive public affairs efforts. I traveled the country addressing social media and public affairs. I worked with and advised a wide variety of federal, state, and nonprofit agencies.

I share this with you to demonstrate the complexity of my organizations and functions. When you toss in political considerations, advocacy organizations, unions, and others, it becomes virtually impossible to "manage" media responsibilities.

Although my title was Director of Public Information for Maryland's largest agency, it was misleading. The bottom line behind that job (and probably yours) is that a wide variety of players had either influence or the final word about what is said to the media and how it is said. Each of the 13 agency heads desired the final say in media relations for his or her own agency. The Department's senior executive, the Secretary of Public Safety, and those on his staff also wanted the final word. To make the situation even more interesting, there were many who often (and eagerly) provided input, regardless of whether it was relevant or desired.

In my conversations with most public affairs professionals, I find that the circumstances described above holds true for them as well. One veteran spokesperson told me that managing public affairs for any complex organization was like "herding cats."

Most of us have endless layers of bureaucracies and connected individuals. It doesn't matter if you're representing a multinational corporation or a local hospital, a public utility or a government organization, the process is essentially the same: a cumbersome bureaucracy and a difficult decision-making process.

The issue becomes a quest to make the organization manageable.

Who is God?

The bottom line for all of us in the public affairs field is first to figure out who influences media-related decisions and to keep that number to a minimum. I refer to this as, "Who is God, and what does God have to say?" Obviously there are others who will also have input, but it's critical to keep this number to a minimum to "manage" the media process.

Many will desire to influence your decisions. Knowing who will give you your final instructions and limiting your "gods" to a manageable number will save your sanity. It will provide you with the best shot of properly handling a situation.

If you doubt that you need to have one central person in charge, try to imagine yourself handling media at a plane crash, during a prison riot, or while you are evacuating a city due to an approaching hurricane (I've participated in all three). Lives and the general or corporate welfare can depend on both accuracy and speed. Handling tough questions or circumstances does not mean that you do not ask for advice from "connected" others. Yes, attorneys have to be consulted. Personnel will want input. You keep important individuals "advised."

But if you include everyone in the process, you will never make appropriate decisions.

There are times when you will need to respond immediately. It is crucial to understand that you need to anticipate the requests you are likely to receive; thus the good public affairs specialist will already know the proper legal and technical advice. That's why public affairs specialists want to know everything about their organization all the time.

Getting Information

One of the best qualities of spokespeople is an insatiable curiosity. They are constantly asking questions about the organization and getting the right answers before a newsworthy event takes place. For example, large numbers of automobile tire failures, major oil spills, or defective or malfunctioning parts suspected to have caused a plane crash would be difficult to research during full-blown emergencies.

Getting crucial information during a major event (especially during evenings or weekends) can be extremely difficult. You need to have information well ahead of time, so you will be ready when reporters come. Remember, if the media do not get their information from you, they will get it from someone else. Getting it from someone else could prove very costly.

A second essential ingredient in successful public affairs is to know when you (as the primary spokesperson) can make decisions on your own without consulting others beyond the senior executive or an on-scene commander. Sometimes circumstances dictate risk and speed. Sometimes, you will have no choice but to respond.

There will also be times when you make instantaneous decisions on your own. For example, you could be at the podium doing a briefing and a reporter asks about a social media rumor (e.g., the local dam is about to break due to flooding, threatening thousands of people). If you are aware of the allegations, and you've vetted them and you know they are untrue, you need to respond immediately. Consequently, you could have firm plans for the media briefing and reporters collectively ask about issues you have no knowledge of. It seems pointless and divisive to drive an agenda they are not interested in. You forgo your planned presentation, access their questions, and promise a response.

Shooting Fish in a Barrel

Members of the media realized a long time ago that organizations can be easily picked apart. It's not that difficult to do. The function or establishment you represent does not matter. Many organizations are terrible at handling or responding to new and aggressive media inquiries. There are plenty of businesses that have done nothing wrong but are incapable of defending themselves. Their response is woefully slow and inadequate. They give the media (and everyone else) the impression that they have something to hide. Their lack of response allows detractors (every organization has them) to speak endlessly and often. Social media blows up and politicians chime in looking to score points with the media and the public.

The Battle Begins

Imagine yourself with a vexing internal problem that is well known to disgruntled employees. Those employees decide to "shop" this knowledge around to the media until one happens to show interest. To compound the problem further, let's say that the major local newspaper embraces the employees. Reporters assigned to the story spend weeks milking employees for all they are worth. It's a lovely arrangement as far as the newspaper is concerned and very common in the media business. In fact, the majority of sensational stories seized by the media come to them through employees or detractors with an axe to grind or an agenda to advance.

So the newspaper reporter has time to develop the story and obtain internal documents. Now the intrepid reporter calls you and announces that her newspaper is ready to run it. All she needs is "your side of the story." She wants your response in two days. How will you respond?

If your organization is like most, you will spend endless hours tracking down executives and experts trying to format a response while your friends in the media sit back and chuckle. They're way ahead of you. They know they have you in a difficult situation.

They are also very aware that this is an extremely dangerous time for your organization. They are fully aware that these are the circumstances that cause "mistakes" to happen. They know that some on the inside are angry that their day or week is being torn apart and that "others" know of the problem. Reporters know that executives are cursing. They also realize that some on the inside are insisting that you stonewall the reporter, that you deny the problem, or that you announce that it's under "investigation."

Other organizations will engage in that time-honored game of "identify the snitch." All of this is a common response to the unexpected media inquiry, and it can lead to the downfall of the organization's leadership if the response is less than adequate or intentionally dishonest.

This is a dangerous time for your organization and a very difficult time for public affairs staff. You have several other media calls pending on other topics. You're trying to arrange and produce television and radio shows as well as a promotional video. Today there was supposed to be a big meeting on changes to your Internet site. There is a lot going on. The same holds true for your executives. How will all of you respond?

An Example

A prison we operated contained approximately 1,000 dangerous and mostly violent inmates. Two-thirds of the population consisted of inmates serving life sentences. Working there was considered one of the toughest assignments in the criminal justice system. It was brought to my attention that employees of this facility were speaking to a major regional newspaper. Reporters were wining and dining correctional officers.

The officers were complaining about items ranging from inadequate training to lousy recruits to salary and overall security concerns. Management had recently cut back on security assignments, known within corrections as "posts." Posts are places in the prison where correctional officers are assigned. The number of posts within the prison affects the use of overtime. Posts were cut to reduce overtime to stay within budget.

When I heard about the reporter talking to the officers, I made inquiries to the prison's executive staff. I was told not once, not twice, but multiple times that the complaining officers were few. I was assured over and again that a handful of employees were complaining solely because their overtime had been reduced. Once I heard that the newspaper was continuing their extensive contacts with our employees, I was determined to head them off at the pass. I urged prison executives to contact the reporter and sit down with her to explain their point of view.

Although I was the "Director" of Public Information for Maryland's largest agency, it was misleading. With multiple agencies, I was supposed to guide them but give them some freedom and flexibility to conduct their own affairs "if" they didn't intrude on the operations of other agencies. If media inquiries involved the affairs of multiple agencies, I took charge of the inquiry. If I felt that agencies were making the wrong decisions, I took my appeal directly the Secretary of Public Safety. Thus in many instances, I "guided" agencies or their full-time public affairs officers rather than give them specific instructions.

A disturbance had occurred at this facility several years back that resulted in the injury of several correctional officers, some of them severely. Since then, the agency worked tirelessly with union representatives to make changes. These discussions produced positive results:

- The number of inmates at the facility was dramatically reduced while concurrently the number of staff was increased.

- A variety of security measures were implemented.

- Assaults against staff dramatically declined.

- Recommendations from outside consultants were implemented.

Staff at the prison were justifiably proud of these actions overall and more than happy to explain their position. So on one fine fall day, prison officials sat down with the reporter. She was relatively new to the paper but was being guided by a very experienced investigative editor.

They provided an hour and a half of explanation plus a one-hour tour of the facility. Although I felt that all of this was a "little too much" (I feared that she would take it as an attempt to intimidate), they did everything I asked. While unsure of what the outcome would be, I believe they did their best.

We Were Massacred

Days later, the resulting story appeared on the front page of the main section of the paper. We were massacred. It was a nasty, bloody story about how correctional officers were afraid for their lives. The article went on to say that as far as they were concerned, citizens who lived in proximity to the institution also were in danger.

A follow-up story appeared within days with members of Maryland's General Assembly calling for hearings. The Associated Press carried the story on the state and national wires. Television and radio stations throughout the country carried the story. It was a bloody mess.

Correctional staff had been sure of their position. They had made changes. They had new data that was presented to the reporter. Staff met with the reporter and answered all of her questions, but obviously, something had gone terribly wrong.

Prison officials had done something that is very common in all bureaucracies: It had lied to itself. The newspaper chose to believe the correctional officers, not us. They offered endless examples of a facility out of control. They provided documentation. It was in the best interest of the newspaper to give a voice to staff if they wanted future cooperation and data, so some negative results were not completely unexpected.

During my follow-up conversations with the reporter, she made it clear that she was turned off by the absolutes provided by prison executives; they would not admit that staff had legitimate concerns. They told her what they told me, that complaints were the result of a few disgruntled officers and that the majority of staff was fine with the operation of the institution. Considering the number of people she spoke to, she believed the complaining staff. Employees made the better case.

It was a dangerous time for the organization because correctional executives could not see the truth; a sizeable number of employees felt that more had to be done and that the recent cuts to posts might endanger their welfare. Prison executives became their own worst enemies.

Within this context, it became easy for the reporter to write a damaging article because she perceived us to be uncaring—or worse—dishonest. So why would good, solid managers with many years of experience allowed themselves to be deceived? Maybe it had something to do with the Smoke Blowers.

The Society of Smoke Blowers

There is a well-recognized society known to public affairs professionals. I have caustically referred to mine as the "Society of Smoke Blowers." All public affairs professionals joke about staff who get on their knees and proceed to blow smoke up each other's derrieres until they are convinced of something that's not true.

Those mentioned in the story I just shared with you are all good and decent people, dedicated servants of the state. They're well educated, successful, and experienced. They are as good as or better than professionals in any organization. Yet, the Society of Smoke Blowers exists in every organization (including the media).

These are dangerous times for the organization. It seems terribly unfair to the executive staff involved. However, regardless of their dedication to their organizations or their employees, some managers seem incapable of crystal clear thinking when caught in the crosshairs of the media.

It's tough to disagree with the Smoke Blowers. As in the story I shared, it's often the case that there are executives who suggest that the complaining employees are few. They insist that the majority of staff surely see the improvements that management has made over the last several years. Certainly the millions of dollars invested and positive change created could not go unnoticed, they reason. Eventually, this point of view influences others. Sometimes executive staff is too close to the subject to see things succinctly.

Some executives embrace the opinion that only a few employees were disgruntled. They are sure that problems presented to the newspaper are greatly exaggerated. Public affairs professionals see this happen time and time again.

In the story I shared, management and I seemed equally sure that reasonable discussion with the reporter would have produced a fair article.

What I Should Have Done

After the article, staff at the Office of the Secretary asked me for an explanation; others held me responsible for a solution. I asked the Secretary of Public Safety for permission to spend a day at the prison to conduct my own investigation. Obviously, something was very wrong, and I wanted to find out for myself what it was, which is what I should have done in the beginning.

The Smoke Blowers continued their ritual dance with greater intensity. They were convinced that the reporter was biased, that she was playing to the crowd, that it was easy to take the side of the "poor, downtrodden" employees against those within the big powerful bureaucracy.

I traveled to the institution and spoke with a variety of correctional officers. It was made abundantly clear to me that they were genuinely concerned about the security of the institution, and they represented the views of most staff. The elimination of security posts to reduce overtime was not the issue. The elimination of posts was symbolic of what they considered to be ongoing problems that threatened (in their opinion) the security of the institution.

Obviously, these were not just a few disgruntled employees. Quite the opposite, they seemed genuine and concerned for the security of the facility and the safety of their fellow employees.

What some within an extensive bureaucracy could not figure out, a relatively inexperienced reporter could. She had spent enough time with enough employees to believe that they were telling the truth and we were not. In her eyes, we had committed one of the greatest of sins: being less than honest, or at best not knowing the true feelings of our own employees. In either case, the reporter felt that the negative article was justified.

Some senior correctional employees had been in opposition to the Smoke Blowers all along, but they were hesitant to disagree when others embraced their point of view. After the article, they came forward with renewed vigor. As a result of calls for hearings by members of Maryland's General Assembly, prison executives asked for a new presentation. They were determined to offer an entirely different point of view. They were not going to be in opposition to the employees. What the employees were calling for was exactly what everyone wanted. Everyone involved, regardless of their job titles, wanted increased training, better recruits, improved salaries and enhanced security. Everyone wanted the same things.

The second article (which was written by a different reporter covering the legislative hearings) was a vast improvement over the first. It was on the front page of the newspaper and documented the fact that there was a unified call on the part of management and labor to improve the security of the institution, and to provide better training and recruitment for employees throughout the system.

It was a much better article because everyone recognized and embraced the truth. It was a better article because we took a long, hard, accurate look at ourselves. It was a much better article because we decided not to lie to or deceive ourselves, and to ban the Smoke Blowers—at least for the time being.

Winning The War

In the introduction I mentioned that the bottom-line advice contained in this book is an emphasis on winning the war, not the battle. We need to examine this concept further.

We're going to lose battles. It will be frustrating and exhausting but nevertheless, we will lose. Those of us representing agencies that carry the heavy burden of policy in practically everything we do will find ourselves at times on the short end of the stick.

The Department handled 150,000 criminal offenders and cases (in prison or on community supervision) on any given day. It was very obvious to everyone that some of our charges would do something wrong, and in some cases terribly wrong.

On the day that I wrote this chapter, a violent criminal serving a very long sentence in a super maximum-security prison had stabbed (tried to murder) a correctional officer. The prison system's public information staff spent the night gathering information and talking to the media.

I recognized that on any given day I could be called into service. I fully understood that the negatives of my job were many. I also realize that there are many agencies that are not significantly different. On any given day, law enforcement or the military will have to explain why an employee was injured or killed in an accident. The teaching hospital will be asked why an improving patient died while under its care. The multinational corporation will be asked to respond to allegations of pollution. The college will be asked to explain the series of rapes on its campus. The local utility will be questioned about long-term power outages. The larger and more complex the organization the greater the chance for challenging media encounters.

Before moving into the specific recommendations on how to deal with these events, we must first recognize that they occur. There is little that you can do to keep negative events from happening. In the best of organizations, bad news occurs. The role of the public affairs official, however, is to keep these events through honorable means from becoming worse.

Keeping it from becoming worse, however, can be far more complicated than it has to be.

The first thing you have to do when bad news hits is to keep your perspective. We within the organization tend to internalize events. We tend to dwell upon the negative as if every reporter and every citizen remember every event forever. They do not. New and breaking stories will quickly replace your "crisis." Remember this and hold onto it as you deal with the latest issue.

How you handle the current event, as negative as it may be, may even enhance your reputation rather than detract from it, as long as the organization has an honorable reputation and does not do anything stupid. This is what I call, "taking a hit."

Taking A Hit

"Taking a hit," means not getting flustered over the current negative event.

"Taking a hit," means not giving in to the Smoke Blowers.

"Taking a hit" means that you have the ability not to make a negative situation any worse than what it has to be.

Those of us who represent cumbersome agencies take painful pride in our ability to "take a hit." We recognize that negative news, like the sunrise, will happen. We fully understand that we do not represent the United Way, the successful local professional sports team or the Sisters of Charity. We know how to "take a hit" because we understand that our objective is to win the war, not the battle.

Battles are an everyday part of our lives. Negative news happens. Organizations can crumble over negative news. I've seen establishments put themselves at risk because they overreact to bad news or they do not react at all or they take forever to craft a statement.

Rather than simply admit that they were at fault (or at least partially at fault) and apologize to the public for their indiscretions, they fuss and fume and fight with the media. Too many top executives feel that their honor or performance has been questioned and will not allow public affairs professionals to put out the fire. They make things much worse than they have to be and then wonder why they are the recipients of widespread negative news coverage.

"Taking a hit" often means that we acknowledge the problem and that the organization will implement measures to fix it.

Move Quickly

I'm not suggesting that organizations take blame for something unfolding where they are not sure of the facts. Yes, it takes time to assess and investigate. Telling the media that you take the situation very seriously and that you are moving as quickly as possible to gather all the facts is fine.

Just move as quickly as humanly possible and be careful not to deny what you do not know.

Yes, I understand that some organizations are unfairly implicated in issues that may not be of their making. If you are sure of your position, then fight back (but please remember the Smoke Blowers).

I do understand that some reporters are unfair. I also understand that we exist in a world that assigns blame regardless as to justification.

Defend yourself if you are truly blameless (strategies forthcoming). You have every right to point out the positives and to make your case to the media and the public. You need to establish your primary communication objectives, and hammer away at these at every available turn.

But you do not have the right to unjustifiably endanger your organization by using inappropriate means to justify your position. I also understand that the main purpose of the spokesperson is to make sure that the organization and its leadership and its mission continues, thus winning the war.

Saving Leadership

Few organizations thrive through constant turnover of senior staff. The confidence that accompanies long-term executives and their multi-year missions are often vital to the well being of the organization and the public it serves. In my 35 years of talking to the media, I have never lost an agency head to bad publicity.

I do not expect all readers to fully accept the implications suggested by making sure that the "leadership" continues. I assume that many would feel that a bunch of bloated government or corporate bureaucrats are hardly worth saving. Sometimes, a change in top leadership is good for the organization, many would assert.

Maybe, but I would disagree most of the time. Assuming that the "leadership" is made up of honorable people with the necessary skills, the organization often takes on their personality and goals. Research is full of examples of successful initiatives that could not be replicated because the key factor was different management.

If you choose all-out battle as your philosophy for every media problem that comes along, then you are going to lose, and you're going to endanger management. The media and the public have little tolerance for those who cannot acknowledge at least partial responsibility, however unfairly you think that the burden is assigned.

Blame It On The Budget

In most agencies, there are budget issues galore. We could justifiably take every piece of negative news and blame it on an inadequate budget or vague laws or an extremely difficult mission or political or shareholder influence, and we would be correct to some degree.

But if the negative news involves the death of a child at the hands of a sex offender (a true story) standing up and proclaiming that the incident is "not our fault" because of the above is almost guaranteed to cause the agency head his or her job.

In many bad news stories, technocrats and others will emphatically insist that the organization is greatly burdened by fiscal, political, economic, and other burdens that greatly hamper their ability to get the job done.

They will assert that the incident is "controlled" by outside forces, so why should they "take a hit?" "When are you going to tell the whole truth about the situation," they ask me. "Shouldn't the public know everything," they assert.

These are appropriate questions that have no clear-cut answers. But in many cases the media are already aware of your issues. Your hospital may be facing a health care problem due to difficulties in recruiting nurses. This issue may not be under your "complete" control due to salary or location factors. Yet ongoing troubles with nursing care at your health center are receiving negative publicity.

It's perfectly justifiable to point out the difficulties in recruiting and retaining nurses and the steps you have taken to rectify the situation. But it's more important to understand the concerns of those alleging inadequate medical treatment and to express sincere sympathy for their plight (even though your lawyers will urge that you say little about the issue due to pending litigation). Pointing out remedies (without admitting legal culpability) addressing renewed efforts to solve the problem and taking responsibility are important ingredients in dealing with the issue.

But who doesn't know that there is a nationwide nursing shortage? Who is not aware that a struggling economy has the potential for hurting your business?

Show me the person that is unaware that lousy salaries make hiring great employees difficult. I do not know of a reporter who lacks knowledge of the major problems facing most agencies or corporations.

But the public and media make the assumption that your leadership knew all of this when they took the job and that it is their responsibility to seek answers and minimize failure within the confines of those realities. Yep, it may be unfair, but it's true. A nationwide nursing shortage may not "technically" be the responsibility of your hospital, yet the media will insist that it is "to some degree."

Citizens, stockholders, and the media will insist that the "buck stops somewhere." "Someone must take responsibility. Someone must assert control," they will say. The public and the media cannot and will not look at it in any other way.

Proactive Media

Perceived accountability is yet another reason not to let potentially negative issues take the public and the media by surprise. Constant dialog with the media and important publics will probably take some of the sting out of issues if they become major news stories.

Proactive placement of positive and even neutral stories about your struggles through social and traditional media provides everyone with a fuller context, thus giving you some control. More on this later.

Honorable executives working hard to find solutions are rarely "targeted" by the media for exhaustive negative news during difficult periods if they are aware of your ongoing efforts.

It's Not Our Fault

The Department of Public Safety worked to enhance health care to female inmates and their newborn children. Regardless of the public's animosity towards people caught up in the criminal justice system, no one would object to better medical care for children and mothers, correct?

It was obviously a win-win situation for all concerned, most thought. I will not bore you with the details, but everything went wrong with the project, and little of it was under our control. All of this was occurring at the time of impending (and massive) budget cuts due to a shrinking economy and tax base. Advocates for the project vigorously fought for its implementation and constantly went to the media with complaints that we were not moving fast enough.

The problem was that some advocates were more interested in the big picture than the legal, fiscal, and community relations difficulties that the program and location faced (community members objected to the presence of the facility).

But it made little sense for us to fight these issues publicly. We "took a hit."

We decided that it was better for us to accept some responsibility for the issue than to point fingers at others, regardless of how justifiable that finger pointing was (yes, I did discuss some challenges with media on an off-the-record basis). We could argue the degree of blame, but we "were" partially responsible for the downfall of the project. The extent was open to dispute.

But we "took a hit" nevertheless. We accepted responsibility because it was in the public's best interest for us to do so. There are times when it's best for all concerned to take some blame, buy time to fix the problem, and move on.

One Spokesperson

I want to return to lines of communication one final time with an emphasis on negative events.

Within any bureaucracy, you have multiple experts and executives who could speak to any topic that your organization faces. But during times of profoundly negative news, it becomes crucial to have only one spokesperson.

In one of the biggest stories I handled, an individual with a long history of sexual violence towards children, was legally released from prison and was under our supervision in the community for less than one week when he sexually assaulted and murdered a nine-year-old child.

I would like to emphasize that no procedural rules, steps or laws were violated in the supervision of the offender. All personnel had operated within existing guidelines. But the murder of a child creates widespread and understandable revulsion. Whether we like it or not, the media and public will assign responsibility for the incident.

There were a variety of agencies that had interacted with this offender and could share "blame." There were local prosecutors who may have failed to pursue all cases in the past. There were treatment providers who could have found a "cure" for this individual. There were judges who could have imposed longer sentences to keep him in prison.

Some of the above decided to point fingers at my organization to deflect attention away from them. They claimed that the offender should have stayed longer or received extensive services while in prison. Many claimed that we should have made better preparations in the community for his return. They felt that we should have supervised the offender more closely during the five days of release.

Again, I emphasize that no laws were violated by my agency, and no rules and regulations were broken. His release from prison was consistent with the discharge procedures of offenders in virtually all prison systems in this country.

His community surveillance was equal to that of other supervision agencies. But others maintained that we could have done better in preparing this offender for his release. Much to the consternation of some within my agency, the critics were right "to some degree." We could have done a better job.

We admitted as much when we recognized two years before the incident that the process of releasing offenders (especially sex offenders) needed improvement. The Secretary of the Department was in the process of implementing a plan.

So we "took a hit" even though we could have argued that no rules or laws were broken in the offender's release. We could have argued that this was the current state of the art in the country. We could have maintained that the budget did not allow for such intensive programming before release.

We could have openly blamed others (the media would have loved the controversy this would have generated). But we did not.

We acknowledged that there were deficiencies within the system, and we were in the process of correcting them. And we expressed great (and genuine) revulsion over the event. Yes-even bureaucrats are allowed to express strong emotions regarding systems that contribute to the death of a child.

Three major newspapers in the market and beyond offered exhaustive analyses of the incident. We answered every question. We did not blame others (although we made sure that reporters were aware of the "full" story on an off-the-record basis). We were polite. We tried to help the media at every turn.

The result was that all articles were extremely fair to our agency. All reports carefully illustrated that a multitude of agencies had contact with the criminal and that all played a part in the offender's eventual release from prison. All mentioned my department's effort to improve the method of releasing and supervising such inmates. It's important to remember that these reporters (and their editorial boards) could have attacked my organization and its leadership. It would have been easy. But all chose not to.

Why One Spokesperson?

As I said, there was an internal debate as to how much of this incident was the "fault" of my agency. There was a multitude of individuals within my Department holding different points of view. This fact alone should make it obvious to anyone that there should be one spokesperson.

Multiple spokespeople offering a variety of opinions on behalf of my agency would have sent many messages to the media and the public. Attorneys and technical specialists, agency heads and influential others had different points of view. But when you go to speak to the media, there should be only one point of view, thus one spokesperson.

Because of the gravity of the story, a national news organization expressed interest in covering it. I already conveyed to them the same information I offered to others. Then the network news producers contacted several agency heads within the Department and asked them for on-camera interviews. Some were considering the offer.

This was a dangerous turn of events. If every agency head decided to speak, there would be a variety of opinions and facts placed before the media. It does not matter how prepared they are. It does not matter if all four agency heads were in the same room at the same time with the same agreements as to what to say and how to say it; some would innocently contradict the other.

The media could create a wedge showing inconsistencies in the story and would begin to examine differences. The organization's position could begin to unravel. There are always different versions of the truth regardless of our determination to honestly answer questions. Confusion over facts is how organizations are injured, and this is how senior staff lose their jobs.

When organizations speak, it is essential that they do it with one voice. Usually, that means one spokesperson. The Secretary of the Department decided that there would be one voice-mine.

Anticipate Negatives

Beyond the concept of speaking with one person, the issues involving the complexity of communication are many.

The essential ingredient is thinking through possible scenarios first, and bringing those scenarios to senior staff for guidance. If you anticipate negative news, then you have an opportunity to sit down with decision makers ahead of time and create understandings.

In some cases, such as potential emergencies, it is important to place these understandings in writing. One of the most important undertakings of emergency management organizations is to conduct drills, evaluate actions and document difficulties and recommended actions.

At times, speed is crucial to your survival. To survive with speed, you have to have a plan in place. You have to know your organization, its data and its people. You have to be ready at a moment's notice.

It is also useful for the spokesperson to be somewhat detached from day-to-day operations. Detachment allows the spokesperson a greater degree of objectivity. Objectivity may, in fact, save the day.

The Perception of Dishonesty

The last major point in this chapter deals with dishonesty or the perception of dishonesty. I have told friends in the media that they are the most suspicious people (beyond street cops or corporate auditors) I have ever met. You could have a reputable organization engaged in an honest discussion of issues and have the whole thing blow up because of "fumbles" that lead reporters to wonder about the purpose or motives of your actions.

An example is the spokesperson taking several hours or days to respond to a simple media inquiry. It leaves the reporter wondering if you have something to hide. Having precise lines of communication and knowing your subject matter well go a long way in combating perceptions of dishonesty. Honorable organizations make honorable mistakes. Honorable mistakes are survivable. What is not survivable is purposeful dishonesty.

Lying

It is inconceivable to me that there are people (in all organizations according to veteran spokespeople) who advocate lying to the media.

Some will criticize me for the use of the word "lie." In their minds, they are simply defending themselves against an unscrupulous media.

Regardless of how it is said and how it is offered, all lies remain lies. Unless you enjoy the prospect of watching an entire organization implode, avoid dishonesty at all cost.

This is said with the full realization that many who read this book will disregard my advice. It amazes me (and many veteran spokespeople) as to how many people think that they can get away with lying.

I guarantee that the media will, in time, discover any purposeful attempt to lie your way through any situation. I guarantee that you will place yourself, senior staff and maybe your entire organization in grave jeopardy (remember all those disgruntled employees?).

Agree to Disagree

But here we stumble into an area that few of us will completely agree on. I believe that spokespeople are obligated to answer questions honestly or to say "no comment" and offer a reasonable explanation as to why you cannot respond (i.e., corporate secret, personnel matter, criminal investigation).

Consequently, I do not believe that spokespersons are obligated to answer unasked questions.

I'm going to offer a very complex example. You could be representing a corporation that is involved in an act of corruption by a senior employee who is charged with thousands of dollars. Your organization has turned the case over to law enforcement authorities, so you are limited in what you can say.

But you and the organization believe in openness and decide to answer media questions about the incident (with the cooperation/direction of law enforcement) and, more importantly, to address future actions to keep this from happening again. You answer every question approved by police investigators.

You did not, however, offer the sordid details about how this person used his position to extort sexual relations with multiple employees. Did you commit a dishonest act of omission? I do not think so.

Your job is to answer questions honestly. You were asked about fraud. For the sake of this example, we will say that the sexual aspect was not an ingredient to the theft. The crime would have occurred with or without the sexual contact.

That, I believe, is a crucial distinction. If the "omitted" act was not a necessary ingredient to the offense, then the spokesperson is not obligated to "offer" this information. However, if the sex act was a component that allowed the crime to take place, then I believe that it should be part of your (or law enforcement's) answers to media questions, especially if the investigation is complete.

Forgiving Mistakes

The media and the public will forgive a mistake (I've made many). The media and the public will probably understand the contradictions of multiple spokespeople during an emergency or breaking news.

They will understand if you quickly point out your own mistakes, apologize for them, and then state the correct the position. But you can avoid all of this by examining your lines of communication, being prepared in advance and keeping your spokespeople to a minimum.

But for media that have experienced negative events with an endless series of organizations and witnessed the missteps that many make while trying to defend themselves, their cynicism seems to have no end. That distrust in many ways is perfectly justifiable after witnessing organizations being clumsy or disingenuous.

A Very Basic Decision

All members of the media must make a very basic decision when covering a story, how vigorously to pursue the issue and your organization. How many stories? How many front-page articles? How many editorials? Do they "go for the throat" or do they "slice it right down the middle?"

Decide to lie or mislead, and you have made their decision for them.

It is amazing to me how fair the media can be if you approach the negative event not only honestly but without fear. This is best done through the reputation you have built for yourself over time.

The bottom line behind this philosophy is the fact that you are an honorable person doing an honorable job, and if you have made a mistake, you acknowledge it and offer solutions.

If you can legitimately build such a reputation for you and your organization, then you have created the best possible defense, the respect of the media and the public.

Veteran spokespeople told me a long time ago that it makes a great deal of sense to think through these issues, to be prepared and to keep your lines of communication crisp, clean, open and honest.

How do you ensure that the circumstances I described do not happen to you and your organization? The chapters that follow will guide you.

CHAPTER TWO: YOUR RELATIONSHIP WITH THE MEDIA

Each of us needs to answer a very basic question: What kind of relationship do you want to have with the media? There are many who believe that they have no influence over media coverage. Others believe that "no news is good news." For example, there are public affairs professionals and agency executives who pride themselves at keeping the media at arm's length. To say that they distrust the media is an understatement.

I know a public affairs executive who is in charge of media and public affairs for a regional hospital. The vast majority of his contacts with the public are based upon marketing strategies he controls such as the purchase of advertising time from radio and television stations. The public is well aware of his institution through these ads. He greatly limits his contacts with news organizations. He does not like or trust reporters. In essence, he has defined his relationship with the media. He is very comfortable with this position and has no plans to change it.

Those who are in control of their own media can survive with this point of view (unless the unexpected happens). I would suggest that most entities, however, cannot. Organizations that handle difficult media situations (or have the potential to experience them) cannot afford to "blow off" the media. News organizations are a regular part of our lives.

What Do You Want?

So again I ask the same question: What kind of relationship do you want with the media? I think I already know your answer. You want fairness. You want accuracy. You want the media to understand your point of view. You object to being treated as cannon fodder. You do not want to be trivialized. You want the media and the public to understand that you are honorable people doing an honorable job. You want the media to publicize your success. You want news organizations to approach negative news stories with sensitivity and an even hand.

We all know what kind of relationship we want with the media. If we are honest enough to acknowledge this, then we need to be honest enough to know what will accomplish our goals. We all will acknowledge that unnecessary confrontations with the media are dysfunctional. The question that I have trouble answering, however, is why so many executives and public affairs professionals seem to be so willing to embrace a combative stance towards the media?

A Badge of Honor

Some executives and media professionals love to tell war stories about reporters who have done them wrong. In my travels throughout the country, the constant theme among some spokespeople and agency executives is their strong distrust and dislike of the media. We wear our descriptions of negative encounters like a badge of honor. We tell each other that we are not true professionals until we have encountered "media hell" at the hands of unscrupulous reporters.

Have I had my own negative experiences? You betcha. I know reporters who claimed exhaustive research but fabricated their data. I know of a case where a reporter stalked a female public affairs professional and used negative stories to punish her for refusing his advances. I know of a journalist who fabricated his quotes (lots of us make this claim).

One time, I had an encounter with a reporter investigating whether registered sex offenders posted on the Department of Public Safety website were living at the addresses listed. In prior cases, reporters would knock on doors to see if people lived at the addresses. They would then turn the list of "bad" addresses over to us for verification. In many cases, the offender did live there, but the person answering the door (often a relative) understandably said that he was not.

A reporter ran the story without giving us the opportunity to check the list first. Quite simply, she made claims that were inaccurate. When we complained, the reporter insisted that she was protecting the people she spoke to. What she ended up doing was providing the public with lots of misinformation. She created a completely unnecessary level of fear.

I could fill multiple pages of this book with examples of journalistic "failings" or acts that I find questionable. So could you. I am also aware of corporate executives who lied to the media. You are, too. We're all aware of our colleagues who have been less than honest.

If you go to a social gathering of reporters they, too, will provide endless examples of corporate, military, advocacy, and government "flacks" who were either too stupid (in their opinion) to know the truth or flat-out dishonest. While we are complaining about lazy, liberal, unethical reporters, they are harping about lethargic, unethical bureaucrats and public affairs representatives.

Media Mistrust-Advocacy Organizations

I spent 10 years in Washington, D.C., representing two entities under contract to the U.S. Department of Justice. One was the Department of Justice's clearinghouse, the National Criminal Justice Reference Center (where I first started talking to the media). The other was the National Crime Prevention Council, home to "McGruff the Crime Dog" and the "Take a Bite Out of Crime" national media campaign (the most successful effort in public service advertising history).

My years in the Washington, D.C. area provided me with my first national media and marketing experiences. Washington D.C. also offered me my first exposure to advocacy organizations.

I do not exaggerate when I suggest that advocates often mislead or flat out lie to the media. I have seen firsthand individuals who have more belief than skill, experience, or training stand before a national audience and instruct them on topics they know nothing about. I'm not suggesting that they were mistaken; I'm asserting that they literally knew nothing about their subject matter.

I wish this were an exaggeration, but it's not. The label "advocacy" does give one the right to express an opinion. That right exists when people providing it have significant experience or training regarding the topic they are addressing. They will also fabricate "research" or purposely skew data to support their own conclusions. The media is abundantly aware of these people and they like or dislike them based upon the needs and prejudices of the reporter.

If the entity is the National Association of Widgets and if the issue is the widget's effect on national public policy, then you would assume that the person pronouncing policy has extensive education and skill in widgets. Often they do not; they are only spokespeople with little to no training regarding the topic they are addressing. They do not have a clue about whether their statements are factual.

Media Mistrust-Agencies Lie To Themselves

It gets worse, much worse. There are people with years of experience in their profession who have never read a research report (not an exaggeration). Understand that every organization (media included) has a stated or unstated mandate to do something. CEOs, agency heads, or politicians set dictates, and they often decide facts and application.

There are few agencies or companies where healthy debates take place about the effectiveness or efficacy of policies and research. While I'll be harshly criticized for this assertion, it remains true. Government, business, and everyone else have agendas and employees either get with the program or they are marginalized or leave. So if the president, governor, or CEO states that red is green, everyone else falls in line. It doesn't matter what the totality of research has to say, they will cherry-pick data from favored researchers (yes, they are there in abundance) and stick to the script. It could be wrong, it could be dangerous, it could cause the demise of the business, but the "expert" will tell you that he has 30 years of experience, and cite data, and tell you that this is the way to proceed.

If you need proof, Google "financial collapse 2008" and spend the next two hours being horrified. "Experts" assured everyone that everything was fine before companies and the economy collapsed.

Cynical Media

We wonder why the media is so cynical. With the demise of experienced reporters covering specific beats (except for sports, technology, and business), how are they to know when an organization is right or wrong? When you have advocacy groups insisting that the research unquestionably leads us to a specific conclusion or when you have an "experienced" expert tell you that something will work, who is there to state otherwise?

More than ever we need a free, experienced, ample, knowledgeable, and aggressive press corps who will say, "Wait a minute. The data you cite is refuted by reputable research or by other experts. Please explain." Beyond the pathetic shouting matches on cable television, that's not happening in many sectors. The media understand this better than you think. They may not have time to pursue it, but if pronouncements don't work, guess who will be remembering the certainty of your answers. The backlash may be ugly.

So What?

I have spent the last several paragraphs establishing the fact that we are suspicious of each other. Undoubtedly, you say you realized that before reading this book. So, what do we do with this understanding?

If you desire fair and accurate media coverage, then you have no choice but to come to a workable arrangement with the media. If you do not have a budget to purchase significant amounts of advertising or are unwilling to pay for and engage in serious social media and website development, then once again you have no choice but to establish a working relationship with the media.

You and your company must choose for yourselves the relationship you will have. You and your organization must choose the data you will use and the efficacy of your pronouncements. The operative word is "choose," because believe it or not, we really do decide the kind of relationship that we have with news organizations. If you decide to be combative or evasive, how do you think the media will respond?

I Can Control Them

Many people think that they can control the media through tough negotiating and setting a demanding tone. They are fooling themselves.

Veteran spokespeople know of respected senior executives who have decades of accomplishments but cannot form a working relationship with the media. It's sad that their mistrust of reporters runs so deep.

For some executives, it cripples them for life. Their negative experiences are so profound that they are incapable of making sound media decisions.

If you do not believe that you can create a positive working relationship with the media, or you think that you can control them, then you should leave public affairs to someone else. Successful media professionals not only know it's possible to establish honest and cooperative working relationships but have been doing it for decades. This point is so contentious for so many. Good media relations do not happen by accident; they are created through hard work and the industriousness of executives and public affairs professionals.

How to Change Their Minds

Experience is the great teacher. I'm not quite sure it can happen any other way. You can tell them that you have decades of media relations knowledge and ask them to consider alternatives but some are often set in their prejudices.

It's been my experience that people with a history of leading cumbersome agencies know better and are allies. They understand the media and are comfortable with the process. They are top executives for a reason.

It's those who have never led who are the most cantankerous. They may be in upper management but they have never been at the top. Now they are. Their mindset is that of someone who has never "crashed and burned." They don't know the reality of public humiliation. They think they can get away with bad, questionable, or overly cautious behavior. All you can do is advise them. You owe them honest answers even when your advice is dismissed or discarded. Be patient. Talk to them. Don't be dismissive of their guidance; they may discover their mistakes on their own. Give solid reasons for trying suggested strategies. If nothing works, then you have to make a decision about whether to stay or leave. Give the process at least six months.

My message to executives? Don't be silly. Your public affairs people are there for a reason. If you are dismissing their advice most of the time, you are placing yourself in jeopardy. Hiring a skilled craftsperson and asking them to disregard their training and experience is inviting disaster. If it's a matter of trust, come to some mutuality agreeable arrangement with your spokesperson and find someone who makes you comfortable. But if you hire a "yes" man who spends most of his time up your derriere, you are inviting disaster. The proverb, "A man who is his own lawyer has a fool for a client," applies.

A Relationship with the Media Is Easier Than You Think

Beyond how to work with inexperienced or combative executives, the first thing to understand in creating a working relationship with the media is that it is relatively easy. There are so many people doing it wrong that you will be greatly appreciated for doing it right. Doing it right means taking a common sense approach to working with reporters. Here's what they want. They want you to:

- Be available.

- Know what you are talking about.

- Have a friendly manner and a kind tone of voice.

- Meet their deadlines.

- Be available in the evenings and on weekends.

- Work for their legitimate needs.

- Provide an honest answer to their questions.

Reporters want the same things that we want: civility, honesty, and fairness.

I had the occasion to work with a spokesperson from the largest sheriff's department in the state. I was always interested by the fact that the media seemed to give him positive or even-handed stories. It was intriguing that he was a new public affairs professional, only on the job for six months. He came to me looking for advice. He wanted to know how to be a better public affairs officer. I told him that he had 80 percent of the game licked. He was a friendly, courteous, and energetic individual whose service-oriented response to the media won them over most times. He worked hard for them, and they in return provided him and his department with fair reporting. I'm not quite sure media relations needs to be any more difficult than the relationship I just described.

After many years of speaking to the media, I have discovered a simple truth in life: It is clearly in your best interest if they respect and like you, and the people you represent.

Do They Like You? Do They Respect You?

When I suggest to reporters that their coverage can depend on whether they like the spokesperson or the organization involved, many strongly disagree. They believe that their reports or articles are based solely upon the issues.

It's insulting to many of them that their reporting could be influenced by the likability of spokespeople or their feelings about the groups they represent. In their minds, spokespeople could be the rudest, nastiest SOBs on the face of the earth, and the organization that they represent could be the International Society of Brutal Dictators, but the resulting article would still be fair, impartial, and above board. Bull-droppings! I have been dealing with reporters for decades. For the most part, I like them. I do believe that most reporters are fair-minded individuals. At the same time they are as human as the rest of us, which means they are subject to the same biases as the rest of us. One of those biases includes our extreme dislike of unnecessarily combative or evasive people.

How you feel about rude and nasty people seems to rub off on the businesses that they represent. If you feel cheated or inadequately served by a car salesperson, you're just as likely to feel that his company is equally disreputable. Why would it be any different for you and the people you represent?

As disagreeable as it will be to some, the likability factor becomes a critical ingredient when you communicate with the media. Many of my friends and associates in public affairs dislike this discussion. They, like my friends in the media, strongly believe that articles and reports should reflect news, not personal perceptions.

I'm not suggesting that relations with reporters should be extremely personal or unprofessional. What I am suggesting, however, is that we need to be advocates for the media when warranted. Often your reputation is based on your willingness to go beyond normal procedures. To put it bluntly, they want access that is usually denied. Choose carefully, but at least consider your options.

Stopping Negative News

Most of the interaction between your agency and the media will take place through telephone calls or e-mails to the designated spokesperson. While it's impossible to describe the interplay and nuances of these conversations fully, both parties understand that much is at stake in each and every interaction.

After the initial pleasantries, the reporter will start asking a series of questions. Sometimes, the questions will deal with potentially negative news. If the spokesperson has done her job, she will have a sufficiently trustful relationship with the reporter allowing her to deny the premise of the question when untrue, thus ending any further inquiries on the part of the reporter.

Deniability may be the single most important function of press representatives. Virtually each working day brings media inquiries that have negative yet exaggerated implications. The agencies we represent have thousands of employees and more than just a couple have "axes to grind." Our organizations are often immensely complex and hard to understand. There is lots of room for conflict and confusion over who we are and what we do. There are endless possibilities for reporters (and disgruntled employees) to misunderstand the business and their point of view, thus endless opportunities for negative inquiries.

Reporters are not going to walk away from the story unless they trust you. Your word is now your bond. To me, this is a profound thought. The fact that reporters would remove themselves from a potential story based on your word is something that needs to be explored.

Timid Responses

In all bureaucracies, there is endless room for confusion. The spokesperson is not going to know every nuance of every aspect of the operation. There are subtleties, inferences, and differences over internal and external research, operations, and many other factors that cause insecurity.

Uncertainty provides inadequate explanations. Many feel the need to run everything by everybody before responding. This situation produces timid spokespeople, and poor responses.

Inadequate replies are often interpreted as the organization trying to "hide something." Skepticism is enough for some news organizations to start investigations and lends credibility to disgruntled employees making negative assertions. If they like or trust you, they often give you the benefit of doubt. If they don't, they won't. It can be that simple.

There is no magic ingredient that solves the problem of likability and trust. Public affairs officers must know as much as possible about their company and its policies. They must have a service orientation to the media and should act as an advocate when warranted.

Media representatives must be bold enough to disagree with superiors. In many organizations the spokesperson finds it extremely difficult to probe policymakers and technical specialists aggressively when the answers they give are inconsistent or fly in the face of public opinion. Yet all of this and much more is necessary if you are to be seen as a credible and trustworthy representative. If you are going to have the ability to stop an inaccurate story, then you must build trust and accuracy in yourself and your business.

The Primary Power of a Spokesperson

Deniability is the primary power of the spokesperson. Many people will not understand this because the story does not appear in the following day's newspaper. To illustrate these results, I provide management with a daily e-mail of all media contacts I receive throughout the day to ensure they acknowledge the unsubstantiated stories we stop. Here are some examples:

- I was asked whether a mid-level executive was fired because of allegations of corruption. My response was that he received a lateral transfer that had nothing to do with charges of wrongdoing.

- I was told that some were strongly opposed to popular legislation regarding sex offenders. In truth that opposition came from another state agency, not mine.

- Sources suggested that one of our prisons was filled with inmates using drugs. We provided data based on extensive drug testing that inmate use of drugs had declined, not increased.

- A source claimed that one of our divisions was discriminating against African Americans. I pointed out that 80 percent of the administration consisted of African Americans and that blacks constituted 90 percent of the workforce. After a review by our equal employment opportunity officer, I told the reporter that the charges could not be substantiated. The reporter agreed.

- A reporter was told that a correctional employee strip-searched a juvenile visiting one of our prisons as part of a group tour for young people in trouble with the law. Reportedly, the teenager was "mouthy." Although he was separated from the group (a violation of policy), no search was conducted.

When you consider that each of the examples could have turned up on the front page of any newspaper or as a story in the evening news, then it seems obvious that having a trustful and respectful relationship with the media can pay huge dividends.

Even when it is discredited, it is still possible for a news source to run the accusation and your response. It happens all the time. I have seen damaging stories and reports based upon much less. But the impact of a potentially negative story is lessened.

How To Make Things Clear

What if events are not as clear-cut as the examples I've shared so far? In some cases, organizations get themselves into trouble because they are unsure of their position on controversial issues. Employees and others can misinterpret the stumbling that all entities go through when trying to make major decisions, and those misinterpretations can be conveyed to the media in damaging and unflattering terms.

A member of the Maryland General Assembly introduced legislation designed to keep sex offenders behind bars for treatment after their initial incarceration was over. As a result of this action there was widespread debate among experts and the public about what the state should and could do to control sex offenders better. Some believed that we should spend literally hundreds of millions of dollars to incarcerate a relatively small number of sex offenders in prison forever while providing treatment services. Others believed that once a sentence is over, the offender has served his time and has completed his obligation to the public. Thus, he should be let go. Some wanted to put the majority of funds toward treatment in prison, counseling, and strict supervision in the community upon release through the use of lie detector tests and satellite technology to keep track of sex offenders.

The point is that there was significant disagreement in the larger community about what to do with sex offenders. Does it surprise anyone that a similar debate raged within my own Department and throughout government? This is when the job of the spokesperson becomes perilous. This is when the public affairs officer learns to trust his or her own instincts and discovers whether they are right.

When top politicians or some in management are offering opinions, you have to listen very hard to what they are saying. You may even have to call their staff and get a more thorough explanation. Within your own organization, you have to question (and sometimes challenge) executives, agency heads, attorneys, and technical specialists. Your top executive will provide the final input, but many players will be determined to "have their say." Throughout this exercise, you will notice a very disconcerting theme; very few executives are completely sure of their positions. There is always an endless array of ifs, ands, and buts.

Results

As I wrote this chapter, I was on the front page of the Metro Section of the Washington Post. The article documents the very clear and precise opinion of my Department regarding sex offenders. We are in favor of tracking sex offenders in the community via satellite. We want to focus our incarceration resources on the worst possible offenders. We state that the dilemma is whether to concentrate on a relatively small number of sex offenders in prison or hundreds of offenders in the community.

The interesting aspect of this position is that no one told me "exactly" what I should say to the Washington Post. My statement was just that, "my" statement. It was a result of careful listening to all the players involved (especially top management) to see if I could gain a consensus opinion. Is this the preferred method?

Many would suggest that the spokesperson (yours truly) could have handled the situation much better. Obviously, creating a working paper containing statements from the agency head and principal politicians for their review would have been much better than interpreting their remarks.

Surely, you say, we should have seen this coming. Many would suggest that we should have had enough time to prepare properly. Well, congratulations on some excellent observations. You're right. This would have been the preferred method.

Endless Competing Priorities

But once again, we had competing priorities, an extremely difficult topic with no clear-cut answers, and limited time to think comprehensively through the situation due to other breaking news.

I would suggest to you that these conditions affect most organizations.

No one disputes that a systematic and careful approach to complex problem solving is the preferred method, but someone once said that when you're up to your navel in alligators, it's a little hard to remember that your objective was to drain the swamp.

Here is where spokespeople earn their money. Here is where they develop their reputation. With any luck you realized that this very hot topic was going to produce media inquiries. You conducted research.

You spoke to the experts. You worked with your top executives long enough to know their preferences. You're also astute enough to understand the priorities and nuances of your top politicians. Thus, you know enough about the situation, the key players, and their preferences to create a correct and meaningful statement.

This Has Something To Do With Trust?

What does all this have to do with the reporter trusting you? The answer is everything. Not only do spokespeople provide statements, they also provide context. Context is one of the most important (and difficult) aspects of answering a reporter's questions. Context means providing the circumstances of the story on an "off the record or background" basis. Without knowing context, the reporter runs the risk of reporting the story inaccurately.

With regard to the sex offender example, I knew the Washington Post reporter fairly well. I had enough trust in her and she in me to take her into my confidence. On a Wednesday evening she asked me for a position statement by no later than Friday at noon. I was not able to respond to her until late Friday evening because my top executives were in meetings. When I provided the statement, I also apologized for the late response. I explained that the consensus opinion I offered was my interpretation of the remarks of many and it had taken time to "get it right." The reporter understood.

I told her that this was the best I could do under difficult circumstances. "Not everyone may agree with everything, but I believe that the statement is a fair representation of their opinions," I said. So the reporter was aware that the state's position may change, and that my statement may be a work in progress.

The article appeared on the front page of the Washington Post. I was very pleased with the results. Because I had enough trust in the reporter, and she had enough trust in me, she wrote the piece fairly.

She conveyed the fact that this was an ongoing story and that some had varied positions. She presented the organization's position as strong but evolving. She left room for change (wiggle room), which was very important to my organization and to me. Everyone involved favorably received the article. Everybody seemed pleased with the strength of my quote and the reporter's conveyance of possible changes in the future.

The story worked because I talked to as many people as possible. The story worked because I had correctly interpreted the desires and priorities of my top executives and leading politicians. The story worked because the reporter had enough trust in me to listen to and understand the context of our position.

Do They Like Your Organization?

Members of the media may like you and trust you, but they may not be crazy about your organization. It obviously makes little sense for them to dislike who you work for. Considering that the very essence of your position is organizational rather than personal relations, it is essential to try to change their minds. If the media thinks your business is a "target" for ongoing negative coverage, then this could endanger leadership. You and senior staff must change their minds. This is challenging to do if the news is frequently negative, but as long as your people are not being accused of illegal or unethical acts, it is more than possible to obtain objective coverage. You need to view this as a long-term project. The benefits will not be immediate.

I assume that you do not represent the International Society of Brutal Dictators. I also assume that you are honorable people doing an honorable job. I realize that within any bureaucracy there are issues better left unexposed, and people who do not improve when in the company of the media. All of that is true in any organization, but you know that you cannot change negative perceptions by sticking your head in the sand.

Go to Them

Your job is to expose the media to your organization and its leadership, mission, and employees. There are an endless number of ways that you can achieve this. Tours of your headquarters or satellite offices by news staff are a start. These trips do not have to be "on the record." Informal discussions with senior staff or technical experts can be useful endeavors.

Keep in mind that many reporters and media management feel at odds with the world around them. They are all aware of public opinion surveys that place them as equals to, or just a few steps above used car sales people. I'm exaggerating, but not by much. You may be very surprised to find that they, like you, are looking for a little respect.

Give them the respect they are looking for. Go to them on your own or take senior staff and technical experts. Tour the newsrooms; visit with the editorial board (more on this later). Be friendly and prove to them that you are all regular Joes and Josephine's. Leave the pompous behavior at home (better yet, discard it entirely). Reporters love to view themselves as the "people's voice." So I would recommend that you be one of the people, not one of "them."

You are Selling People, Not Products

What you're trying to do is to break down preconceived notions about who and what you are, but the media is not going to interact with the widgets you make or the social plans you create. They are going to work together with you and your people.

The trick in all of this is to get management to relax. If you and your entourage are genuinely friendly, then the media representatives you seek to influence will be gracious in return. It does not have to be any more complicated than that. The purpose for meeting the media is to improve relations. These trips are not designed to bring up old grudges or to provide you or staff with a forum for complaints. Like any other social interplay, pleasantries must be exchanged and working relationships established before the hard bargaining begins.

These meetings are not one-way trips. If you go to them or they to you, it's done because both of you want to come to a better understanding of each other based upon meeting each other's needs. You need to come to that agreement internally before meeting them. Meeting needs means providing access. They will expect as much accessibility as possible. The bottom line is that you are going to have to give a little to get a little.

Convincing media representatives that your organization is ethical, humane, and hardworking and that you operate in the public's best interest are vital ingredients to obtain fair news coverage. If you portray yourself as honorable people doing an honorable job under extremely difficult conditions, the media and public may even grow to like you. But once again, you will earn the news coverage that you choose to obtain.

CHAPTER THREE: THE ART OF THE INTERVIEW

This chapter discusses strategies and issues that promote or hamper the exchange of information. We need to have a thorough examination of both, and it needs to address everyone in the decision-making process.

I said in the introduction that an increasing number of inquiries are being made through e-mail and text messages and that some in the media are increasingly comfortable with a text exchange. But I believe that conversations are often in our best interest. There will also be times when text inquiries will be discarded and phone or in person conversations will be required.

There are two kinds of interviews: prepared and "O my gawd." The prepared interview is self-explanatory. The "O my gawds" are much more interesting. There are common characteristics to both. Interviews are filled with subtle nuances and inferences that make all the difference in the world. The exchange of information can almost be secondary.

In one example, a reporter from a national newspaper called to ask about castrating sex offenders. I knew the reporter from a variety of prior contacts. She stated that a member of the legislature proposed that this method was a justifiable approach to the problem of sex crimes and criminals, and she wanted our reaction. I asked to go "off the record," and she quickly agreed.

"Okay, Susan, how the hell do I respond to this one?" I asked in mocked exasperation. "I don't know," she laughed. "I think that it's funnier than hell."

We both agreed that the research indicated that the process of castrating a criminal does not remove his sex drive or his ability to commit a sex crime. She stated that "just because you chop off the caboose doesn't mean the engine stops running."

"That's it," I proclaimed. "That's our quote!" We both enjoyed the exchange, but then I asked, "Susan, do you really want a quote from us on this?" Susan replied, "This is ridiculous. I'll ask my editor. If we need a quote, I'll call you back." That was it. I never heard from her again on this subject.

What I learned from Susan is that she did not have a personal investment in the story. I was able to discuss research pertaining to castrating sex offenders on an "off the record" basis without committing my department to a rather awkward public statement.

But another reporter may have a personal investment in criminal castration and take the story very seriously. With a reporter like that, castration is nothing to joke about. He or she will want a formal statement and will expect it by the deadline. Thus, we have two reporters covering the same story with two entirely different points of view. What happens may depend more on the information the reporter offers to you than what you give to the reporter.

To be successful, we need to be aware of the subtleties. Public affairs is not harpooning whales; it's more like fly-fishing. There is a grace inherent in the listening skills involved.

Another issue is that you are "artfully" selling yourself, your trustworthiness, and the organization's reputation. Obviously, this approach does not apply to every media request, but it can apply to many. The most important attribute is our ability to be friendly, helpful, accurate, and reputable, thus having the capacity to influence the story.

It is that ability that makes or breaks us as public affairs professionals. There are a multitude of ethical methods to provide us with the capacity to influence the story, thus the reason for this chapter. If you approach every interview with the same energy and creativity you offered during your first date with your spouse or the first time you met your in-laws, you will do just fine (hopefully with better results than with the in-laws).

The point is that interviews are a stage, and you are the "act." Interviews are not forums for dishonesty, but they are platforms for energy, creativity and knowledge. Shakespeare said, "All the world is a stage." Nowhere is this truer than in media relations.

No Fear, No Hostility

I frequently see the "No Fear" corporate logo for Nike. The mantra for public relations professionals should be "No Fear." I sometimes think that the advice offered to me about dealing with dangerous dogs applies to many reporters; they both smell fear and take it as an opportunity to attack.

The opposite approach is equally damaging. Too many of us start media conversations with subtle or overt hostility. I will suggest that if the reporter is clearly annoyed or personally invested in the story, then you have just set yourself up for a negative interview.

Some public affairs people do not return phone calls or e-mails or respond late in the day. Do you think this conveys a message of fear? The same applies to always asking for media requests to be written. You are selling yourself as much as you're presenting a point of view. If your attitude is one of fear, apprehension, or hostility, the reporter may assume that you have something to hide or that negative accusations are correct.

In a variety of disciplines, I have advised people to trust their instincts. Well, I'm not quite sure that advice applies to everyone making media decisions. Although successful public affairs professionals constantly rely on their instincts, many individuals within the organization seem to go haywire when confronted by the media. To some, their instinct is to run or hide. Obviously, this leads to difficulties.

Common Courtesy

Each interview should be approached in a genuinely friendly and civil manner. Whether you know the person or not, common courtesy applies. Use the journalist's name. If you know his or her nickname or any appropriate personal information, use it! However, I am not asking you to fake it. I am not suggesting that the interchange be insincere. If you feel uncomfortable with this approach, then don't do it. I was raised with the idea that it was mannerly to engage others in conversation and that it was perfectly acceptable to inquire about their lives. I do not want to suggest that courtesy is solely a tactic. It's preferable to be appropriately friendly, and it's a wonderful icebreaker.

Comment on the journalist's last report or article. Reporters like to talk about prior work and the challenges involved. Humor, preferably clean, can be useful. When you are selling yourself, you need to find a style that you are comfortable with that expresses your individuality, sincerity, and helpfulness.

The world is filled with well-dressed people with big smiles and friendly handshakes who seem to personify insincerity. What people are looking for is the "real thing." Be that person. Express genuine sincerity and do it in your own style.

There is a reporter (now an editor) for a major newspaper who is well known within his organization for not wearing socks. The reporter could call with the most damaging of inquiries, and my first question would be, "Bob, are you wearing socks today?"

Bob's usual response would be, "Sipes, it's none of your damned business if I'm wearing socks." I would then swear that his co-workers told me not to answer any questions if he was not wearing socks. I stated that I was in complete solidarity with his fellow employees and their objections to the unpleasant habit. At this point, he would threaten to put the socks in an unpleasant place, and the interview would commence. Obviously, the point has nothing to do with whether Bob was wearing socks. Rather, it has everything to do with establishing a personal (if not bizarre) bond at the beginning of the interview. Yes, you can only do this if you have a prior relationship. Don't attempt it if you are uncomfortable or unsure.

If the reporter is from out of town, I'm going to ask her about some characteristic of her hometown. It could be the weather, sports, or anything else germane to local conditions. The topic doesn't matter. I have had five-minute conversations with complete strangers about our families and children. I am not disingenuous. I would like to think that I'm just trying to be mannerly.

Starting off each conversation with something other than annoyance is important. If the reporter does not smell fear at the beginning of the interview, then you are more likely to have a successful exchange of views.

Combat

Quite frankly, some reporters look forward to a combative exchange. Many of us seem more than happy to play into their hands. Nothing makes it easier for the television station or newspaper to slam you. I have been in newsrooms when a reporter puts down the phone and announces to his editor and those around him that the spokesperson is "being a jerk." Combative spokespeople play into the hands of those who feel that we are nothing more than unprincipled flacks.

Like the Smoke Blowers described earlier in this book, the entire newsroom then gathers in a large circle and proceeds to blow smoke up each other's derrieres until all are convinced that the spokesperson and the associated organization cannot be trusted. All the negatives inferred are now strengthened. Everything your detractors are saying gains greater importance. The editors and reporters are now convinced that you are trying to hide something.

Sometimes reporters will purposely try to provoke you. I know of journalists who start off some conversations as if I have kicked their family dog.

She begins with, "God, Leonard, your people have really screwed things up this time." She says it with the gusto of a plane approaching the airport. "Well, Kate, you obviously intend on writing an article without hearing our side of the story," I say, thus challenging her journalistic integrity.

At this point, Kate advises that she has a source providing negative news. So the dance begins. I remind her that I have served her long and well and that I deserve better than an attack conversation. I state that she needs to hear our side before coming to any conclusions. Kate then settles down and starts listing issues that need response, and I begin my work. Before we end the conversation, however, I obtain a pledge that she will wait for my response before she makes conclusions. She always agrees, and then I set off to "make the day" of my superiors.

For some spokespersons, a conversation that starts off with nasty accusations creates a tailspin from which they cannot recover. The spokesperson goes to his or her boss and those standing nearby announcing that the reporter is being a jerk and has information that the organization is doing something "terrible."

Every Smoke Blower in the area now performs their ritual dance. "The media are scum," they all chant in unison. Candles are lit to ward off evil spirits. Goats are slaughtered. Then the agency head or someone else of importance loudly proclaims that he or she is not to be intimidated by some horse-faced reporter. The day will not be completely rearranged because of one reporter's hostile inquiries. Therefore, deadlines are not met; the reporter and editor are convinced that the organization has something to hide, and the article is damaging. Senior executives from the home office call to find out "what the hell is going on?" Then, all sit down and wonder why the news is so negative.

Why Is the News So Negative?

Perceptions of media fairness hamper our ability to respond. Our executives and others need a common understanding about what constitutes news.

Some believe that news decisions are made on the basis of what will bring a profit to the newspaper or television station. "News organizations are profit-making entities," they assert. "They do what is in their economic best interest." Reporters believe that accusations of "selling" their work solely or partially as a moneymaking enterprise is insulting in the extreme. The reporters I know find the charge revolting. As always, the answer lies somewhere in the middle. I have found that the majority of reporters are ethical people who do their jobs based mostly on the evidence at hand.

Newsworthy articles and reports are like the Supreme Court's definition of pornography; you know it when you see it. The adage of "man bites dog" rather than "dog bites man" constitutes a common sense definition of "news."

The normal workings of government or business are not news. The unusual or negative typically is. Regardless of the profit-making motives of news management, news is news. Most of what graces the front page of the newspaper or acts as the big story on the evening news fit into the category of unusual or negative. A government's new program to ensure that drug treatment is available to criminal offenders is news in the beginning. A problem reaching that lofty goal is even bigger news.

The big fire is going to make the front page and will headline the evening news. To many in the industry, news is news, regardless of the economics involved. Reporters will insist that they are merely reporting facts; let the chips fall where they may.

What the Public Wants

There is often another twist to this discussion. The news is often negative because that's often what the public wants. There was a story about a young woman found dead a mile from my home. It seemed that everyone in my neighborhood followed the story carefully. Individuals may not say that they prefer negative news, but they infer as much by stating in surveys that they want information on crime, accidents, fires, or bungling on the part of government or corporations. They will say that they want information that is interesting or affects their daily lives. Well, most of what affects our lives is negative.

Positive news may be nice, but in the minds of many consumers, it's not "news you can use."

Every newspaper that devotes itself to soft community news is inevitably small and local. As much as some commentators lament the unceasing coverage of crime, accidents, fires, and the usual investigative reports, the public desires this information. Therefore, these types of events are featured as the "big story" on the eleven o'clock news.

We Contribute to Negative News

I spoke to a retired editor of the Washington Post over lunch long after a series of negative reports about the National Zoo. The coverage at the time seemed endless. What prompted such a series of hard-hitting articles about a zoo?

There were legitimate questions about operations and the welfare of animals, and there were insiders who were willing to produce documentation and context. However, the real reason for the continued coverage was that zoo officials were insultingly uncooperative with regard to answering questions. Their responses were hostile and stonewalling in nature. After a series of articles that could only be described as scandalous, zoo officials raised a white flag and began to provide answers. The series of negative reports came to an end.

Are You The National Zoo?

We know that the most negative media inquiries will come from employees or those with opposing agendas. These individuals will often pass on internal memos (typically written in the usual imprecise bureaucratic style) that leave virtually anything open to interpretation. Here is an important point to remember: all internal correspondence should be written with the media in mind.

Giving information to reporters provides a great deal of power to those on mid to lower rungs of an organization. To many employees, this is the only way they believe they will be able to influence organizational or public policy. They believe that the media forces change or ensure that things will be done differently. Often they are correct.

The news is negative because of the nature of reporting and informing by employees and others, and because of our overprotective responses. By the time the Smoke Blowers are done with the public affairs professional, their instructions are often guaranteed to produce a dysfunctional response and a guaranteed confrontation.

Our replies are sometimes so vague and bureaucratic as to be practically meaningless, and some reporters enjoy "punishing" the organization for perceived dysfunction. Some technical or legal specialists advocate fuzzy, formless answers. Many spokespeople encounter individuals who embrace being vague and obscure on a regular basis. They will claim that they are simply trying to be "accurate." They are indifferent to the fact that the interaction produced hostility or distrust on the part of the reporter or editors. They simply don't care; it's not their butts on the line.

Snatching Defeat from the Hands of Victory

I dealt with a reporter who is a hard-charging individual known for doing her homework and asking very tough questions. We were at the final stages of approximately twenty telephone conversations taking place over the course of two months. She had an inside source making exaggerated accusations about the previously mentioned release of a criminal from prison and murdered a child. I felt convinced that I had spent enough time with the reporter to convince her that the inside source had exaggerated his story. Virtually all insiders overplay their hands when talking to the media.

I was convinced that much of her original premise had been discredited. She had final follow-up questions for some previously interviewed technical experts who now expressed concern about further conversations, demanding that she place her questions in writing. They further asserted that the questions had to be such that they could respond to them in one day. They were tired of the process. The reporter expressed surprise over the indignity of submitting questions in writing. She wanted to talk directly to the experts. She immediately became suspicious of the request.

"Okay Leonard, what the hell is going on? After meaningful discussions, your guys suddenly want to play hardball?" she said.

It was a dumb move on our part. My inability to convince bureaucrats of the dangerousness of their stance proved costly. She now wondered why we suddenly had become so protective. What should have been one report now had the potential to become two or three.

She was also in communication with a national network representative expressing interest in doing the story. The double indignity was the fact that we were mostly (but not completely) innocent of the insider's claims, but our lack of a personal response raised suspicions that we had something to hide. We had taken a partial victory and discarded it.

It's difficult enough that the news (under the best of circumstances) is going to focus on negative events. It's hard enough to deal with the never-ending flow of overly aggressive reporters, but many spokespeople feel that the hardest part of the job is dealing with bureaucrats inside the organization. We often "choose" the media we obtain. If we choose to be unnecessarily combative and negative, we will get negative news in return.

Strategies for Dealing with Negative News Inquiries

So, now you are prepared. You understand the interview as an art. You know why news is often negative. You know how to take a hit. You have your lines of communication in place. You've done your research. You understand that your mission is to win the war, not the battle. You know how to deal with the Smoke Blowers. You understand that you control your own destiny. So what do you do when the negative media inquiry comes?

"O My Gawd" Interviews

All of us get media requests where we are unprepared. There is only one solution; don't panic. Remember that the majority of negative media inquiries come from exaggerating employees or other "knowledgeable" sources. Their charges are usually much worse than the situation actually is. Your goal is to get through the day as honestly and ethically as you can while understanding that you do not have a complete understanding of the issues at hand. "Buying yourself a day" is a common tactic. You want to get through the day without making the situation worse.

After you have been through unexpected interviews twenty or thirty times, you begin to take them in stride. While not being complacent, you understand that the story, upon investigation, is uniformly not as bad as it appeared. It will still result in a negative report or article, but you know how to take a hit. Sometimes, the worst thing you can do under these circumstances is to overreact to the story. Be professional in your attitude. Get as much detail from the reporter as possible. Find out the deadline. Contact your executives immediately (yes, we all know they are busy) and get them working on the case. Answer the who-what-when-where questions to the best of your ability.

Questions that come in by noon and are answered by early afternoon have a greater chance of being dismissed by the media, but please note, allegations that take all day to assess or disprove may be used. The space or airtime has already been assigned. They have, in their view, almost no choice but to use it.

You Are Not Obligated To Do Their Job

You are only obligated to answer the questions asked. You are not obligated to do the job of the reporter. You will rarely encounter reporters who are intricately knowledgeable of your operations. The vast majority of reporters are "general assignment," which means that one day they are handling a fire, the next day a traffic accident, and the following day, your organization. Most reporters, even those who have some knowledge of your business, will not know enough about the details to ask specific questions. They are essentially on fishing expeditions; they are not sure of their questions.

Don't be surprised when radio and television reporters bring in a copy of the newspaper containing the article generating widespread interest. That article (and the biases contained within it) is often the sole research used by many non-print reporters. This situation will prompt "big picture" questions. Reporters will look for themes that the average citizen will respond and relate to. Knowing this, you need to be prepared with answers that respond to the "big picture."

Let's say that a report has been issued on the status of widgets and their relationship to food safety. The 250-page report is extremely technical in nature, which means that the average reporter will not read the entire report or understand it. The report attacks your organization either directly or through inference. You represent the National Association of Widgets. Hopefully you have read the report and talked to your technical experts. If not, read the executive summary and get a technical expert to explain the rest. Do not talk to the media without the best possible understanding of the situation or results of the research. Get in touch with your senior executives; know your organization's position.

The unprepared reporter, however, is most likely going to focus on "big picture" questions. They want to know if your widgets are having a detrimental effect on food and public safety.

Remember, for unprepared interviews you simply want to get through the day without making the situation worse. Develop four or five major points to convey. They are known as your "overriding communication objectives." Most questions should be answered with elements of these objectives.

You're not obligated to answer every vague and offbeat question directly. You're not obligated to help reporters form their questions. It's perfectly justifiable to answer "big picture" questions with prepared answers.

You can take control over any interview by having new facts and figures or unique research at hand. If it's truly timely and unique, lead with this information. Sometimes it's interesting to the point where the person conducting the interview lets you go where you want to go. This tactic works only within the context of the situation, and only you can decide if it's worth using.

Beyond your opening statement, stick to your script. Keep it honest and simple. Keep your overriding communication objectives in mind, and you will do just fine.

Here are some examples of communication objectives based on the example above:

- We put customer safety first.

- We are very proud of our product. It has an excellent track record.

- Independent, outside evaluations give our product very high marks.

- The International Association of Widgets reviewed our product. We exceed their standards.

- If we have any indication that our product does not meet standards, then we will recall it immediately.

- Nothing is more important to us than the loyalty of our customers or the safety of the public.

- We invite the public to contact us at our website, via a toll-free number, or through social media. We will respond to all inquiries as quickly as possible.

Now, if you do not put customer safety first, or the International Association of Widgets has not reviewed your product, then don't say it. Just in case you believe that you can get away with saying it, remember those disgruntled employees? You think you're in trouble now? Wait until they are done with you. Honesty will always be your best policy. Having a script of prepared answers to help you "stay on message" is of immense help, especially if you are doing multiple interviews.

Please remember, however, that answering all inquiries solely with "canned" responses on subsequent days is a sure-fire method of proving to the media and the public that you are less than honest. Sincere questions deserve appropriate answers. There is nothing wrong with taking questions you cannot answer and providing responses later in the day or the following day. It's perfectly fine to admit a lack of knowledge and a need to research the situation, especially on the first day.

Beyond "O My Gawd" Interviews

The rest of this chapter focuses on basic characteristics of day-to-day interactions. While everything in this chapter is interchangeable, it seems simpler to address prepared interviews separately. For day-to-day interviews, you have a good understanding of the characteristics of your organization. You are aware of your policies, research operations, legal issues and the preferences of leadership. You also have a decent awareness of your detractors and the reasons behind their concerns. You are knowledgeable of your lines of communication. Media inquiries are expected and understood. In this scenario, little takes you by surprise.

Being Understood, Being Direct

Every time you create your primary communication objectives, try to think of your audience. When I'm creating answers to potential questions, I run them by my wife and trusted friends. I do this because I want to know how the average person is going to respond to my answers. I want to communicate to a very general audience, the same audience that the reporter also wants to influence. If my communication objectives do not resonate well with the general public (they sound like a pompous bureaucrat), then a reporter and the public may see this as an insincere response.

The public is suspicious of bureaucrats or corporate officials and their vague and technical answers. My goal is to respond in a way that can be clearly understood. I am not going to resort to jargon or legalese. Reporters and the public do not appreciate, nor will they accept, purposefully vague answers especially when their questions pertain to personal or public safety. You need to have basic themes in your arsenal of answers that honestly defend your position and resonate well with everyone.

Being Vague

I am going to contradict myself somewhat and suggest that there are times when vague responses are appropriate, depending on the accuser, reporter, or audience. There are stories that hit like hurricanes, and all you can do is hang on and see what unfolds over the course of days or weeks.

If you are debating someone who is employing unfair tactics, then I believe that it is ethical to respond "carefully." Advocates are known to "advocate," and to some of us, this means that their assertions are less than honest. Talk show hosts can be unfair. Reporters can be biased. Sometimes, the question is so general that it's impossible to respond directly. There are times when the story becomes so intense, and the accusations so strong, that you are uncertain of what to do.

I'm not suggesting that you engage reporters in battle. I am saying that there are times when generalities can be a useful part of your strategy. For example, you could be asked about a mildly embarrassing but wildly exaggerated event brought forward by an advocacy group. The group has handpicked the reporter because she shares their views. Rather than respond directly, you might say, "Well, based on a preliminary review, the charges seem unfounded, but we are very concerned about the issue, and I can assure you that we are looking into it." Your quote is not going to stop the report, but you probably avoided a dispute over details that have the potential for providing additional coverage.

Please remember that fair questions deserve equitable answers. However, there is no obligation to respond directly to questions that are purely self-serving or ridiculously general. Smile and be polite in response, but generalities are sometimes necessary.

If you are debating issues with advocates during a talk show, and they are deliberately unfair, you are not obligated to comply. Remember, they are trying to get your organization to do something. That is their only objective. If they have to "stretch the truth" to do it, they will. Here is where your communication objectives play an important role. Stick to them. If asked about your factory dumping thousands of gallons of raw sewage into a stream and it was only fifty gallons that you promptly took responsibility for and initiated an immediate cleanup, you are not obligated to participate in an unfair debate.

The purpose of the advocates is to enact additional laws to protect the environment. It's a noble purpose but not at your public relations expense. They are trying to make an emotional point that resonates with the public's suspicion of corporations. If it's a stretch of the facts, then so be it. They believe that the end justifies the means. If you quickly point out that it was fifty gallons and what you did to rectify the situation, they will insist that it was much more than that and therefore your response was inadequate. They know that the public has no way of knowing the truth. The host may know that your accuser is wrong, but he will insist that it's not his job to take sides.

I would state the truth, but I would suggest an immediate launch into everything your corporation is doing to protect the environment. "We are committed to the environment!" you insist. "We spent over ten million dollars last year retrofitting smoke stacks to produce clean air," you assert. You then continue to focus on what you want to talk about rather than give in to blatant unfairness. Politely but firmly stick to your communication objectives. Take control of the interview. Choose the moral high ground by insisting that you and your organization are staunch supporters of environmental issues.

I do not advocate vagueness or combat for the vast majority of questions or interviews. Yes, I realize that it is easy for bureaucrats to read unfairness into a question and automatically lapse into generalities. Yes, politicians use this tactic all the time and get away with it.

Politicians Can Stretch the Truth, But We Cannot

Politicians love "intangibles," which are "themes" without specifics. They will stick to the big picture, especially during campaigns. As spokespeople, we need to recognize that there are different rules for politicians and us. Reporters know that they can be full of "hooey," but they expect this. Political campaigns are filled to the brim with assertions that resonate with the public but are misleading. They will promise the sun, the moon, and the stars but promise not to raise taxes. It's impossible to do any of this, but in that world, it's acceptable behavior.

The media will try to substantiate or deny many of these claims, but political advertising can be overwhelming. Say anything often enough and it has a way of sticking. Society accepts this as standard operating procedure.

While some spokespeople admire the aggressiveness of politics, we should not be confused over what they can do (and get away with) and what we can do. But there are times when circumstances dictate general responses. Having your communication objectives in place and knowing when to be direct or evasive are sometimes necessary for survival. Like everything else in this business, it's a matter of context.

But I repeat that honesty, simplicity, and directness will save you most of the time. Envious of politicians? Then join them. But they can do what you cannot.

The Straightforward Approach Is Best

Handling media under difficult circumstances is part art and part common sense. There will be many within your organization or from the home office that will encourage you to use a variety of strategies that would make Machiavelli proud. Examples include offering the response hours after deadline (or not returning the call at all) in the hope that the reporter will lose interest. Another includes the insistence that the journalists read a complicated court decision or a very technical document as the sole method of response. A third may include the suggestion that you simply lose the reporter's requests and blame it on the demands of the day.

All of these suggestions range from silly to dangerous. Most reporters are fair-minded individuals who simply want to do a job ethically and without unnecessary effort (with emphasis on unnecessary). If reporters begin to feel that you are purposely "screwing" with them, then your goose is cooked.

Reporters talk to each other within the same newsroom and within the same market. It will not take long for them to come to a consensus regarding you and the organization you represent. If they believe that you are purposely trying to make life more difficult than it has to be, then you will find that your organization will be targeted for some nasty media. It amazes veteran spokespeople that some will advocate a disingenuous approach yet complain bitterly about the result.

Spin

A great example of this is the term "spin." I often have individuals ask me how I intend to spin the story. They assume that I'm devious enough to know how to create a message that changes the story. I constantly hear about "spin doctors" and consultants for corporations and major political organizations who are responsible for the "spin of the day." All of this suggests that we can control the media through what we say and how often it is said.

Most of us are not major political organizations with millions of dollars to spend on advertising. We're not multinational corporations buying up advertising space during the Super Bowl who get to tell a story in the way they prefer. For the vast majority of us, all we have is our credibility and reputations, and I have yet to see any organization "spin" its way out of an intensely negative story. If our reputations for honesty and fairness precede us, we have the power to influence. If we are trusted, we can deny negatives. "Spin" infers a power that no one has, and even if "spinning" was successful for an incident or two, sooner or later it will backfire.

Being Brief

I like to use "sound bite" because it conveys to my co-workers the desire to take complicated issues and break them down into simple and understandable phrases. I'm not being devious; I'm being clear and concise. There is a huge difference.

The longest any response should be during an "on the record" electronic interview is twenty seconds (half that is preferable). Breaking your thoughts down into ten to twenty-second bites is useful in answering questions during any public engagement.

Abraham Lincoln had a simple yet direct strategy during his delivery of the Gettysburg Address. Lincoln followed a world-renowned speaker whose speech lasted hours. Lincoln's address lasted minutes. No one remembers what his predecessor said. The world celebrates Lincoln's address. Emulate Lincoln, and you will do just fine.

Simplicity Is Next to Godliness

Lincoln was also known for his plain speaking approach to dealing with practically any subject. Lincoln knew how to communicate; he was honest, direct, and to the point. He was also a very effective storyteller. Yes, even Abraham Lincoln had his communication objectives and hammered away at them at every possibility. Lincoln also had his fair share of complaints about the newspapers of the time. To Lincoln (and to all of us) simplicity is next to godliness. Keep your statements and communication objectives clean, simple, honest, and direct, and deliver them in like fashion.

There really isn't a creative or strategic approach in dealing with the media. We cannot fool them forever. The straightforward method is best. The most effective strategy is being helpful, friendly, and knowledgeable and communicating in a direct and simple style. Some aspects of media relations have no mystery. You try a simple and direct approach and ordinarily the media will try to be fair in return. It does not have to be any more complicated than that.

Finding the Right Words

The straightforward approach often means finding words that you are comfortable with. For many of us, words that end in "ly" are agonizingly difficult. For some, the difference between "antagonize" and the far more complex "agonizingly" is immense. Try to find an array of words that fit you as comfortably as your favorite pair of jeans. Stick to them. Please do not be like some who feel compelled to send listeners and readers to the dictionary; they seem to take great comfort in their ability to confuse. They are not successful communicators.

The very essence of public affairs is the ability to communicate crisply and cleanly. To accomplish this, you need to find language that is comfortable for both you and your audience. Respond appropriately to your listeners, but in ninety percent of your public statements, leave the difficult words at home. While many will suggest that this is part of the "dumbing down of America," I completely disagree.

Finally, please avoid organizational jargon at all costs. No one will understand the terms that are unique to you and your organization. If no one understands them, then it completely defeats your communication objectives to use them.

Finding Your Comfort Zone

All of this comes under the heading of finding your comfort zone. The words you use, how you dress, how you feel and how comfortable you are with your subject matter are important to your psychological well being. Try through trial and error to find your comfort zone. Remember what makes you feel good. Then try to emulate these circumstances as much as possible when doing future interviews.

Answering How or Why Questions

One of the most difficult inquiries to answer are "how or why" questions. Answering questions about who, what, when, and where are easy; they all pertain to the basics of any event. It is the "why" question that frequently gets organizational representatives into trouble. The "why" question pertains to the motives of your organization. The motivation for the organization's actions will often define the story.

There are few media reports without input from those who will profit from your dilemma. These individuals include competitors, dissatisfied consumers, angry stockholders, advocates, union members and many others. Any or all will try to shape the story in a way that benefits them. Rarely do detractors contact the media to defend your organization. They do not call to rave about your intricate quality control standards or your dedication to customer safety.

They do not convey the contextual information of national studies that indicate that one out of every 100,000 cases of widgets will have problems. They will imply negative motives. The fact that a case of defective widgets made its way to the market and is suspected of causing health problems is difficult to handle. Reporters will ask you how or why this occurred.

Thus, answering the "why or how" question becomes paramount. The public is aware that mistakes will happen within any large organization, but everyone recognizes that few will accept deceit. There's clearly a huge difference between making a mistake and the purposeful dumping of the case of defective widgets into the public domain.

So it becomes obvious that you will be asked the "why or how" question. Why did the organization create the case of defective widgets? How did this happen? Is it a case of purposeful sabotage? Did your organization violate industry standards? Did you know that the case of widgets was defective before it was introduced to the public? You must create an answer that is simple, honest, well documented, and resonates with the public.

Some people in public affairs will suggest that you not answer the "why" question. They believe that they are just too dangerous and difficult to answer. I strongly disagree. Your persona must be that of an honest individual doing an honest job in service to the public. Anything less than this plays into the hands of your detractors, provides ammunition to those in the media who question your motives and convinces the general public that you have something to hide. Answering "why or how" questions simply and directly is a crucial element in any successful media interview.

Unreasonable Deadlines

Do not be intimidated into meeting unreasonable deadlines. If you do not have a copy of the 250-page report in question, then you are under no obligation to respond until you've had a chance to read it and discuss it with your technical experts and executives. If a reporter calls at three o' clock in the afternoon with a deadline in two hours and you are unprepared to answer, then don't. Ninety-five percent of the telephone calls into my organizations are answered on the same day, and virtually all deadlines beyond that are met. Even if an inquiry comes in the late afternoon, I will make every effort to meet the reporter's deadlines. If I am not prepared to provide an answer that is honest and meets the organization's objectives, I will not respond.

Hopefully, you have enough of a relationship with the reporter and the people they represent for them to understand that it is impossible for you to meet their deadlines. If they do not understand, that's tough. You have an ethical obligation to try to answer questions in a timeframe they desire. You are not required to do the impossible.

Buy Yourself a Day

There will be times when it is clearly to your advantage to "buy yourself a day." I mentioned it earlier in this chapter, but it deserves more attention.

A reporter called from a wire service to get our comment on a report from the U.S. Department of Justice stating that there had been a dramatic decline in the success of criminal offenders on community supervision. The editor was told by the "Justice" spokesperson that we had supplied the information, as did all other states. "If it's your data supplied to a reputable organization, then you should be able to comment on it," he said.

The problem was that the individual responsible for supplying the information was on vacation. You will find that within all organizations; there are experts who know a great deal about individual issues, but no one else is equally knowledgeable. Many assume that their supervisor or others in the unit also have the same knowledge. Often they do not.

The media call came late in the day and I made every attempt to research the issue and respond. I did not want my organization to suffer potential bad news without a response. As I found out, without that key person, no one knew the "real" reason for the decline. By the time I responded to the editor, he told me that he was stuck; he had space to fill and had to run the story.

I did the best I could under the circumstances and provided reasons for the decrease that seemed to make sense. I was also aware of other research indicating that the success of offenders on community supervision had declined, so I felt it was reasonable to respond. When the expert returned from vacation on Monday, he explained that the decrease was a result of an obscure change in the law. "It wasn't a real decrease in success of offenders," he explained. "It was just different numbers based on a new law."

I should have bought myself a day. As soon as I found out that the expert was not available and that others were unsure, I should have insisted to the editor that we were not in a position to respond. If the editor persisted, then I should have appealed to someone higher. Against my better instincts, I did the interview. Sometimes it's better to push the media inquiry to the next day when it's ethical to do so. A day can buy you a lot of wisdom. A day can also bring new stories that cause the reporter to completely lose interest, especially if you push the story to Monday (thus buying yourself a weekend).

Responding in Detail

Some organizations try to be disingenuous by responding to questions with referrals to confusing tactical or legal documents as the organization's "sole" response. I think reporters can figure out when you are helpful or not (although they have a much more colorful term for it).

It is, however, perfectly justifiable to use your website or technical documents to respond to some inquiries when appropriate. Posting documents on your web or social media site can also be of immense assistance when you are dealing with multiple requests for the same information. Some media inquiries and ninety percent of student or public requests are nicely handled through this method.

There is nothing disingenuous about responding in great detail to a reporter's questions or providing technical or legal documents. After all, you are simply responding to their inquiries and it may be the best response you have. Sometimes, it's clearly in your best interest to answer in a very detailed way. Just be prepared for follow-up questions.

Writing the Reporter's Story

We return to the theme that many reporters lack specific knowledge about your organization or the incident or report in question. Reporters (like everyone else) are subject to information overload. There is a point where some will give up trying to understand what they are reporting on. If you have established a relationship of trust with the reporter and the news organization then some reporters will allow you to "explain" the situation to them. You get to clarify the report, background, and context. In essence, you get to write the story.

This is an opportunity for you to ensure that your message is accurately conveyed to the public. While you are under no obligation to provide answers to unasked questions, you are ethically obligated to respond to specific questions truthfully and accurately. For an opportunity to define a story or issue, you are responsible for being fair and accurate, telling both sides even if it plays against the organization you represent. Nevertheless, within that balanced, truthful, and accurate response is an opportunity for you to get your organization's message across.

While media managers will be horrified by the prospect of a bureaucrat defining a story for a reporter, it happens all the time. I find that even experienced reporters who have come to trust you over time will depend on you to characterize the issues. Please, if you get the opportunity to do this, do it fairly, accurately, and honestly. Give both sides. Develop an unimpeachable reputation for fairness. It will pay dividends in the long run.

Tell a Story

I was called downtown early on a Sunday morning to handle a near escape from a maximum-security institution (the corrections spokesperson was unavailable). The criminal was a person with a long history of violence. A correctional officer apprehended him as he jumped from a wall and hit the sidewalk. Here was a criminal who worked for months making tiny bits of progress in order to escape. He put himself in great danger as he pulled himself out of his cell, which was several stories above ground level. He pulled himself through layers of "razor ribbon" to get to the roof and then began his dangerous decent to the ground.

I had to decide on the issues to focus on as the media arrived. I could simply stick to the basics of the incident (who-what-when-where, etc.) or I could tell a story. I decided to do the latter. With all the drama I could muster, I explained the account of the near escape, the chase, and the heroic capture of a dangerous criminal by a correctional officer. I told the story accurately and ethically, but I added a different perspective. The media decided to cover the story the way that I explained it.

Sometimes you must decide for yourself that a glass is half full before someone else decides that it's not. Sometimes it pays to employ a little bravado and tell a story.

Changing Direction

Discussing a variety of topics in an interview can lead to some interesting results. The subject may be tough as nails, but you may hit upon something unexpected that resonates with the reporter. You could be discussing the decreasing price of widgets, and the reporter seems very interested in the fact that you ship a million widgets a day to cities throughout the world. Then, go with the flow. Extend the conversation. Offer him the opportunity to go to your distribution center. Make your chief of transportation available. You never know which way an interview will go. Always be willing to move in a direction that benefits your organization and the reporter.

Your Boss Talks to the Media

Early in my career I was warned by veteran spokespeople that some in the upper echelon would talk to reporters without telling you. Executives within the organization will use the media to disagree with agency heads or CEOs. They will use reporters to communicate to the rest of the organization when they believe that this is the only way that they will be heard.

The ability to influence the media means power to those who feel outside of the decision-making process. This happens at all levels. Remember this when you're viciously badmouthing a journalist to a high-ranking person. I once complained about a nasty encounter with a reporter to a group of executives. Two weeks later, the reporter gave me my statements almost word-for-word. I told him that he deserved the remarks, and I had a right to be angry. He just smiled.

With regard to top executives, I was told by a member of the media of an administrator within my department who spoke to a favored reporter, and the same reporter would contact his spokesperson for an official statement. The agency head never advised his press representative that he was talking to the reporter. I told the spokesperson what was happening. She was very hurt and saw her boss in a different light thereafter. I know of nothing else that could possibly place a spokesperson in greater jeopardy.

It's my opinion that the executive who seems to exhibit the strongest anti-media feelings is usually the one talking to reporters. Additionally, I've done follow-up with reporters after a major story and learned that many executive staff for an agency in my department spoke to them off the record. This was conveyed by a variety of reporters. Sometimes it's not a matter of who is talking, but who's not.

Don't Blow Off Knowledgeable Reporters

If a reporter tells you about a negative issue within your organization and provides sufficient detail to back it up, you can assume that there is at least some validity to the accusation. It's not unusual for you to be on the receiving end of a negative inquiry and know nothing at all about the circumstances being described. You must respond in the only way you know how, honestly. Deny direct knowledge and promise to research it. Never deny what you do not know. Never make a blanket statement that the question is without foundation. You may find your denial in the headline of the morning paper only to retract it when you discover that the accusation not only has merit, but is also true to some degree. Being forced to retract an earlier statement is highly embarrassing, and it has the potential to damage your public affairs career. If you do not know, then say so.

You're Not Aware

Those of us in public affairs often lament that we are the last to know the important stuff. Executives at all levels hide damaging material and issues from spokespeople all the time. It's obviously better for you to know everything, thus you have the opportunity to be prepared. Even when there is a trusting relationship between spokespeople and executives, they believe that it's in your interest not to be told.

In any organization, it is not unusual for information on important projects to take weeks or months to reach you. Sometimes information does not get through to you at all. Technical experts will purposely withhold information. Research staff will keep tough news quiet.

We often say that information is power. Well, there are people who realize this and use the information they have only when it benefits them or their part of the organization. These "information hogs" will not provide data or knowledge of the incident until it suits their purposes.

Your Boss Doesn't Know

Even more startling is the fact that your top executives are often unaware of negatives within their own organizations. People who run agencies and subdivisions are not anxious to inform top executives of wrongdoing or mistakes. Even executives at the highest levels of the organization get misled; what they get is often sugarcoated to deflect personal blame.

It is not unknown for the agency spokesperson to get an inquiry from the media, and that inquiry is "run by" the executive with the assertion denied, only to be retracted when it's discovered to be true. The agency spokesperson must learn to play detective. We must be realistic about the information that flows (or does not flow) to us.

If a reporter offers you details, check it out with those closest to the action before going to your executives. I have been the bearer of bad news to multiple executives, none of which had any prior knowledge of the information I was sharing. Going to the technical experts or mid-level managers first gives them an opportunity to "fess up." I remind them that not coming clean after the reporter's accusations would place themselves as well as the executive in jeopardy. If I went to my boss first, he wouldn't have the knowledge to respond and his probable inclination would be to deny.

That's why the spokesperson needs to keep her options open and personally investigate potentially damaging stories. After several of these episodes, the Secretary of the Department of Public Safety began to see me as more than a spokesperson and gave me unfettered access to everything and everyone in his agencies. I became a member of the Secretary's personal staff because I was there to protect him from the media, and his own people. News representatives began to understand this relationship, thus my word was trusted as being the best voice of the agency.

Your Experts Make Mistakes

When negative events occur, it is your job to consult the right mix of technical experts, attorneys, and mid-to senior-level executives to understand the issues properly. But one of the dilemmas is that key people make mistakes. Attorneys apply the wrong laws, technical experts misunderstand operations, or your executives are confused. This is a dangerous moment. When negative news is breaking, especially if it's coming fast and furious, I have found that people make basic and fundamental mistakes (especially if key people are unavailable). To put it bluntly, they give you wrong information. It's obviously a very difficult situation, but you need to be aware that it happens. Veteran spokespeople assert that it occurs more times than you would think.

I have had executives who have calmly and dispassionately provided what they think is true, or offer what they wish was true, and have it turn out to be completely wrong. To be caught in the glare of media exposure is not a pleasant experience. Like the proverbial deer in the headlights, senior executives and technical experts can freeze. Fear does little to induce clarity. These individuals have trained themselves to display a very cool and calm demeanor regardless of the circumstances. It can be very disarming when they are sitting there serenely providing you with the wrong information. When media questions about a negative event are coming fast, the possibility of misinformation is high. Because the information is coming from an executive does not mean it's correct. Just because the legal opinion comes from an attorney does not mean it's accurate. This is why the spokesperson spends a good deal of time learning about every aspect of the organization and its operations.

You need to ask hard questions. You need to ask the same questions that any reporter would ask. Sometimes, you need to be tactful, yet forceful in the questioning of technical experts or executives. Like a good reporter or detective, you're going to uncover discrepancies in any story. In fact, others within the organization may tell you that the information you have received from executives is flat out wrong. Keep this in mind as you progress throughout your career. Treat all well. You never know who will be in a position to save you.

My executives, the organization, and I have been saved multiple times by a low-to-mid-level employee who came to me and said that false information had been provided. I had senior employees strongly assert a position, and we were ready to proceed when someone from the research department gave me data that completely disproved their hypothesis. You cannot afford to ignore divergent points of view. If you receive an opinion from an executive but are told by a technical expert that he or she "simply does not understand the situation," then you cannot use the information until the discrepancy is resolved. You must have the courage, tact, and will to solve this issue before moving forward.

Put the two or three individuals who are offering different opinions in the same room. Once again, with all the diplomacy you can muster; lead them in a joint discussion until a consensus is reached. You may have to go so far as to tell a very important person that others are questioning their views. This is a very difficult and somewhat dangerous time for the public affairs person. These high-powered individuals do not take kindly to a discussion involving mistakes.

Do individuals purposely lie? In my opinion, most do not. While I do not think that it is common under stressful circumstances for an individual to lie, it is not unusual for them to tell you what they think you want or need to hear.

Beware of the easy explanation. Be cautious of the solution that fits your circumstances like a glove. If it sounds too good to be true, then it probably isn't true. Your best defense is to be aware that it happens.

The Reporter as Digital Detective

Some reporters are extraordinarily good detectives. Today's journalists are armed with an incredible array of computerized tools. I have made it quite clear that reporters are fewer in number, and they often don't have a clue about what they are reporting on. However, there are still journalists who are skilled, aggressive, and computer savvy. Bloggers and podcasters are some of the smartest fact finders out there. There are times when they are better prepared with facts than mainstream reporters. Regardless, all have access to a wide variety of public and private databases that provide answers to many questions. Anything that is publicly (and privately) available is stored somewhere. Today's search engines are powerful tools bringing research, previous stories, context, and personal information to anyone in seconds.

Private organizations collect information and provide data in a searchable format for a fee. If you have purchased a house or a car, then virtually anything involving that transaction, including your home address, social security number, credit rating, unlisted telephone number, income, family members, and other personal features are probably in somebody's Web-based service. Don't underestimate the ability of a reporter to find information about you and your organization in seconds in private or public records.

Most privacy concerns are directed towards government, but your Internet service provider, Facebook, other social media sites, or Google have more personal data than the National Security Agency ever dreamed of. Spend time searching for information about your executives and your organization. Use Google Alerts to keep track of what's being said. Paid media and social media monitoring services are expensive but better.

Let executives know that media has access to the social media accounts of those they are interested in. In a day where the most common computer password is "PASSWORD" or "123456," do you expect your executives to understand the privacy implications of their

Facebook accounts? Your executive is writing friends on social media about how this idiot reporter is investigating the organization when the account is marked public, thus the "idiot reporter" is reading his remarks that day.

Reporters will search databases before coming to you with questions. In addition, most negative news stories stem from employees or detractors providing internal documentation. Therefore, reporters may be very prepared before they pick up the phone.

Like all good detectives, savvy reporters will already know the answers to some or half the questions they will ask. They will use these inquiries as "lie detector" tests to establish your veracity, as well as the facts. Your objective is to ascertain the knowledge of the reporter and whether the allegations are true. This analysis is ordinarily done during off-the-record exchanges. It is crucial for you to establish the extent of their knowledge and resources when you brief your executives.

I acknowledge that this can be difficult. Some reporters do not want to "show their hand" too soon, if at all. Others, quite frankly, do not care and will describe what they have in detail. A few will lie about what they know, which makes the assessment even more difficult. I try to answer several questions first as a sign of good faith before asking for their information. Obviously, they will not reveal names, but it is common for reporters to state that they have been talking to employees or others and have documents. In fact, it's common for reporters to fax or e-mail me their documentation. There have been times when a reporter will e-mail an internal document or research report before I can get it from my own organization.

As previously stated, everything written in any organization should be created with the media in mind. Everyone should ask themselves, "How would a reporter interpret this e-mail or document?"

Informants

I make it a rule never to try to figure out who is talking to the media. I am so used to others talking that I take it in stride. If this individual is discovered, then someone else will probably take their place. It's pointless to try to establish their identity, and your media source will punish you if you do.

Your ability to understand and assess the situation accurately will be crucial to the speed and precision of your organization's response. It's also fine to convey this to the reporter.

If a reporter tells me that she has internal documents, I try not to sound too impressed. "Okay, join the crowd," I say, "but I have a lot going on today, so you're going to have to give me some details if you want me to put this at the top of my list." If the reporter gives me details, and it's serious enough, I will pull executives out of meetings. If not, then I will write an e-mail and people will respond when they get my message.

It's amazing how this reality prompts reporters to be more forthcoming. They know that employees and detractors often "shop" the same information to other news outlets, so they would like a prompt response. I simply tell them that they "have to help me help them, so tell me as much as possible about the information you have." Many times they do.

I do not want to oversell the issue of preparedness; some reporters do little homework before asking questions. Some reporters' sole source is the morning newspaper or the wire story. Well-prepared reporters usually represent regional newspapers and big-market television stations. Within every television or news-oriented radio station, several investigative reporters will be equally prepared. The majority of reporters will follow the lead of the investigative journalists; thus, it is very common for those reporters to influence the entire media market.

Wiggle Room

Your job is to provide "wiggle room" and as much flexibility as possible for your executives. If a reporter asks you to provide the completion date of a project, and you were told that the date is May 1, then I would suggest you say that the project will be completed early that summer. Better yet, convince your executives to provide you with a date or circumstances that everyone can live with and stick to.

Remind them that many pronouncements never seem to come true. Everything in government or business is flexible except our executives. They see themselves as "in charge" of circumstances.

I have seen times when an executive sets a date for the implementation of a major project and announces it to all concerned. Yet the technical experts insist that it cannot be done by that time. I would return the executive and inform him of the discrepancy, yet he will once again tell me that the date is accurate. The technical experts are equally adamant that it is not. I was once caught in the middle and was blamed by the technocrats for creating a problem (I guess they believed they could blame me but not the boss)!

My "assumption" in all of this was that the executive was sending a message to the technical experts to meet his deadlines. The technical experts were also sending a message to the boss that her deadlines were impossible. Most public affairs professionals tell me that this state of affairs is not unusual.

Is a "wiggle room" response disingenuous? It's possible but far more preferable than providing firm responses to circumstances where the results are unclear (quite frankly, the circumstances are always unclear).

Reporters may hold you to your pronouncements. It is possible that negative articles will result when your stated circumstances are not met. The best alternative is to explain the difficulties involving the "fluid" nature of your enterprise. As always, honesty is the best policy.

Providing accurate descriptions of the delays (i.e., weather and construction projects) may buy the additional time you need while keeping the media informed (thus the beauty of extensive off-the-record conversations). Once again, if you are seen as a reputable and helpful spokesperson, you might have enough credibility in the bank for them to give you the benefit of the doubt. You have to become knowledgeable of the circumstances to be seen as a worthy spokesperson. You may have to devote a considerable amount of time to the project to understand and explain it fully. Some in the public affairs business call this "dancing around the issue." Well, in my years of talking to the media, I have done enough to dances to make the Smoke Blowers envious.

Do your best not to put your executives and organization into a corner with no room to turn or change their minds. Be both ethical and flexible with your answers.

Hardball

Despite everything that I have said about minimizing confrontations with the media, there are times when you have to play hardball. There are reporters without ethics. There are editors who assign conclusions to stories regardless of the facts. At times, reporters fabricate data. There are news people who will embrace every negative assertion by every employee regardless of the ridiculousness of the claims. There are also members of the media who will not give you or your organization an even break.

The "hardball" strategy does not apply to one story or a reporter with credibility. Everyone is entitled to "bad days." Even the best of journalists get stuck with assignments where management is being stupid. We know how to take a hit. Let's not overreact to difficult circumstances. If wronged, then discuss it directly with the reporter first. If that does not work, go to management. State your facts and observations plainly and dispassionately. Do not lose your composure. Understand that they make the final decision, and you may lose the argument. If they know you and trust you, you will get a fair hearing and some consideration.

If you are on the receiving end of blatant unfairness over a period of time, then you may have a "different" relationship with a reporter. This is done with full knowledge that higher-ups within the news organization will probably back the reporter before they back you.

What do I mean by "hardball"? First, it does not mean that you refuse to answer the reporter's questions. The vast majority of us, in both the public and private arena, are "obligated" to respond to questions posed by the media. It is in our organization's best interest. But the reporter will get nothing else beyond a very precise answer. I will not provide context, off-the-record explanations, or any elaboration whatsoever. If I have twenty media calls on a hot topic, then guess who will be the last to be called? Needless to say, this tactic should be used very rarely and saved only for the most unethical of reporters.

Note that there are some in my profession who believe that my version of hardball hardly fits the criteria; they refuse to respond to the reporter in any way. In my years of service, I have done this very infrequently. I often say that we should not take hostages. I remind everyone that we're ethically or realistically bound to answer questions. This tactic is also guaranteed to produce negative news, so your executives need to be aware of the strategy. Sometimes, unethical reporters give you no choice.

You're Nervous?

Understand that you're going to be nervous during media interviews. I am greatly appreciative of top-notch spokespeople who will fully and freely admit that nervousness comes with the territory.

I have done far more interviews than most spokespeople, but a certain amount of fear always remains. I was so nervous before my first radio talk show (the most popular in Washington, D.C.) that I thought I would be unable to go on. I did. I was fine.

When you stand before a television camera or sit behind a microphone in a radio station, you're going to feel something ranging from a twinge in the stomach to mild panic. There are existing materials that address overcoming the nervousness of public speaking, so I will not try to deal with all of the various strategies here. What is important for you to acknowledge is that even in seasoned professionals, the nervous stomach remains.

Try not to become complacent when the nervousness subsides. I have done thousands of interviews only to find myself on live television experiencing a small panic attack.

I once went into a television studio to debate the member of a union who was making disparaging remarks about my organization. I did fine. The producer invited me back two weeks later to do it again on another topic. For whatever reason, when the red light on camera two came on and the host started asking questions, I felt an unanticipated nervousness that caused me to fumble through the interview.

I have done lots of live and taped interviews since then, and I have done most of them successfully because I acknowledge the possibility of nervousness and prepare for it ahead of time. I find that holding my breath and counting to ten before I slowly exhale seven or eight times immediately before the interview works wonders. Extensive practice is your best defense. Sometimes I pretend I am an overly confident person giving a speech or doing an interview. My practice sessions are my scripts.

Think that this advice is strange? Well, did you ever watch a famous actor being interviewed? Some of them are terrible! While on the big screen, they are great. Without a script, they stumble and sometimes stumble badly.

Get yourself a script. Practice your lines. The principal "panic" time is when you begin. Smile to yourself, recognize the moment for what it is and continue. The initial 10 percent of your interview, speech or talk show appearance should be scripted. It's not necessary to do this word-for-word. Having key words or themes can be enough. But the most important thing to remember about being nervous is that few who see the report or witness your address will notice.

I have given speeches before hundreds of people and I was so nervous that I thought for sure that it would be noticeable. At the end of the speech, many remarked at how good it was. You are never as nervous to others as you believe yourself to be. While you are sure that you're making a fool of yourself, you're not. Try not to be hard on yourself when you feel that sense of panic. You may notice it, but in all probability others in the room will not. Even if they do, they will recognize something of themselves in you. Acknowledge your nervousness. Your audience will often rally to your support.

Sometimes, television stations will need you to go live. The interview may be on the street, in the studio, from a remote news desk or a variety of other places. Benefits of going live include the ability to make your points without interruption or interpretation. Sometimes, that objective is worth the risk.

Feeling Alone

Many times, unsettled or nervous feelings may be caused by internal disputes. You are told to do something stupid by superiors, and you cannot ignore the instructions.

When receiving silly or incorrect instructions, it may be hard to live with yourself and your own reputation due to doubt in your position. It's hard enough to do this job without the distractions of internal disputes. I do not know how to solve this problem beyond the fact that I try to blend what the reporter is asking for with internal directions. Neither is getting exactly what they want, but it's my job to forge a middle ground that all can live with. You are trying to win the war, not the battle. You may be the only one in the room at the time who understands this, but that's the nature of the job. Now go get a drink and a good night's sleep. Don't kick the dog.

It Can Get Worse

I would be less than honest if I did not admit to having followed disagreeable instructions to the letter. The Secretary of Public Safety once derisively asked me if I knew how to follow any instructions at all; this occurred when we agreed to disagree about how to proceed. There are times when you have to carry on as instructed. Sometimes I'm pleasantly surprised with the lack of fallout, and sometimes I accurately predict a train wreck. And yes, there have been times when an experienced reporter will observe that my response was unusually silly and suggest that I must be following bad advice.

"Having a bad day, Leonard," one editor opined when his reporter was frustrated with my response.

"No comment," was all I said. He decided not to use my original response.

It's not the first time a member of the media understood unspoken circumstances and let it pass. Once again, your reputation precedes you and sometimes allows a benefit of doubt. The issue was revisited the following day and consequently, the Secretary had a change of heart. Buying yourself a day is just not a tactic for media relations. Sometimes it applies equally to internal advice when cooler heads prevail.

Practice

Practice, practice, practice! I know it's going to sound ridiculous, but the bathroom mirror is an excellent substitute for an audience. Debate your spouse. Argue points to neighbors. Take public speaking or acting lessons. Make sure that your primary communication objectives (nice and tight and clean) are understandable to a larger audience.

Take out instructional material from the library. Find material on the Internet. An excellent tactic is to conduct the debate in your own head. Debate your employees. Have them play the "reporter from hell." Encourage them to use every unethical tactic possible. Record the session. Recognize that you are not only testing your communication objectives, but also looking to see how well you appear on camera.

Whenever an agency head or a technical expert is going to do talk radio, I sometimes grill that person until they are comfortable with every conceivable negative question. I teach them how to fall back on prepared communication objectives. I cannot emphasize enough that your best defense in conducting any interview is to practice. Do your research, but the most important thing is your ability to test your strategies and themes with someone else until you are personally comfortable with the results.

The Sound of Your Voice

Get used to the sound of your own voice. I have witnessed spokespeople who are fine addressing small groups but feel strange when addressing a larger audience. It wasn't the size of the audience that mattered as much as it was the public address system. It can be weird to hear your own voice coming back at you in real time.

The same thing applies when you are doing talk radio. Using headphones and hearing your voice in real time takes getting used to. When I do talk radio, I wear the headphones around my neck at all times unless forced to put them on to hear listeners' questions. Even then, I only use one ear cup at a time to minimize the distortion of hearing my own voice.

Radio and Television Reporters: Fairer Than You Think

The majority of radio and television reporters will go out of their way to make you feel comfortable. For most television journalists or those conducting talk-radio shows, it makes them look good to make you look good.

If you stumble while filming a taped interview, television crews will stop and allow you to try again. The radio reporter doing a recorded telephone interview will let you do the session over until you feel comfortable with the results. The talk show host will often treat you like a guest and may protect you from unreasonable callers. Needless to say, this treatment is afforded to novices and people they perceive as cooperative and honorable. They have to interview you in the future and they, like you, are looking to develop goodwill.

Combative individuals and those representing scandalous stories will not receive the same treatment. You should never count on these courtesies for every interview.

All of us have a horror story etched in our minds of a local camera crew running after someone for an "ambush" interview. You see the reporter banging on the door of a home or the window of a car trying to get quotes. These examples are exceptions, not the rule. In thirty-five years of talking to the media, I have never experienced an ambush interview.

You should never be off your guard. The obvious danger of a television interview is that the crew is in your office, and not on the telephone (yes—you can invent an excuse to get off the phone). Reporters will always ask for ten minutes and stay thirty or longer.

Camera operators will often tell you when the camera is on or off, though you should ask to be sure. However, they rarely remind you that the microphone on your lapel was on 10 minutes before and 10 minutes after the "formal" interview. Most people in the media relations field will tell you that the interview is never over until the news crew gets in their vehicle and leaves.

Offer to carry some of their equipment to the elevator or ensure that their parking pass is stamped or walk them to the front door. You would be surprised at what a little courtesy can do for good relations.

Be Careful with the Nationals

These observations, however, do not always apply to national or international television and radio crews covering tough issues. Local media try not to burn bridges. They know that they will return for future interviews. They may need you far more than you need them. National reporters do not hold similar expectations. They can afford to be as aggressive as they want to be. You may never see them again. With national media, you have to prepare for the most difficult of interviews. Be especially wary of the magazine format "news" shows.

You have four primary forms of defense when dealing with national crews: endless preparation, filming them as they record you for your own protection, choosing not to do an interview, and issuing a written statement. If you are defending yourself during tough times, and you have done interviews with local affiliates, then there may not be a reason to grant an interview to a national network crew. The network can always use local footage. They will assure you of fairness and try to convince you that it is in your best interest to do an interview, but you have the option not to participate.

Be especially wary of the celebrity reporter. Those "nice" producers will set the stage, and the celebrity reporter will arrive thirty minutes before the interview, typically proceeding through a series of tough questions on prepared three-by-five cards. Out of forty-five minutes of recording the reporter will use three for the final product. Generally speaking, the result is not flattering. Written statements are useful tools when you have a reason to mistrust the "celebrity" reporter or the magazine format news shows. Sometimes it's just better to respond in writing when the results are almost guaranteed to be unfairly negative.

Usually I am a strong advocate of participating in all interviews. This is my one of my few exceptions. Some "nationals" choose to embrace every possible negative regardless of conflicting evidence. If the results are pre-ordained, it seems to make little sense to participate. If they care enough about the issue, then they may try an ambush interview. If they do, smile and tell them to contact you at the office and arrange a time for an interview. You may want to reconsider, but a well-written statement is usually enough to forestall this event.

I am not trying to portray all national reporters and crews in a negative light. The overwhelming majority of them are honorable people doing an honorable job. Most were friendly, cooperative, knowledgeable, and fair.

I had a crew from ABC Evening News spend an entire day at a jail and not do a story when they found that the advocacy group making charges about "mistreatment" of juvenile offenders had overstated their case. This is exactly the opposite of the argument made previously that economics drives news coverage. It cost ABC News an enormous amount of money to send a crew of four people and not file a story. When making a decision about doing an interview with a national television news outlet, I would suggest that you watch their program and call people they interviewed. See if they received fair treatment. Be guided by their statements.

Moving at Media Speed

One of the major problems for public relations people is that they move at the speed of media when everyone else in the organization is moving at the speed of a bureaucracy. To fully understand the media is to recognize that their entire existence is defined by the noon news and evening deadlines. Can you think of anyone within your organization who accomplishes a variety of tasks every day by a certain time? Can you think of anyone who is willing to do this 365 days each year?

The above paragraph provides much of what we need to know regarding the built-in friction between bureaucracies and the media. The media is mostly made up of type "A" personalities. Newsrooms are filled with demanding managers who insist that stories and the accompanying interviews, photographs, and research all be accomplished in very neat and tidy time frames.

Now we can visualize the struggle that spokespeople go through every day of our working lives. Hard-charging type "A" personalities are picking up the phone and calling you, insisting that you research a very complicated subject and have the answer as well as somebody to interview by no later than three o'clock that afternoon. While the media moves at a hundred miles an hour, we move much more slowly. While the media demands speed, the bureaucracy insists on a slow and deliberate course of action. This is why many in the media find it so easy to "pick off" organizations and their slow-moving ways. The mere fact that we have organizations traveling in two different directions and speeds should be enough to explain this dilemma.

Our understanding is that the media provides "the best available version of the news." It is abundantly obvious that journalists cannot provide every story and meet every deadline with one hundred percent accuracy. But the media, like every other organization, is scrutinized and hounded by the public and their fellow members of the press.

Every day, thousands of citizens and competing journalists take great delight in pointing out informational and grammatical mistakes of the media. Members of the media fully understand that they are in an extremely competitive business. They see themselves as having no choice but to move with speed. The quicker they can obtain and analyze the story, the greater chance they have of making fewer mistakes or misinterpreting the data. Needless to say, the quicker they get the story, the greater their chance of beating the competition.

How Do You Move with Speed?

How do you move with speed when your organization does not? Basically, you must have a supportive bureaucracy and executive staff that will allow you to make decisions while consulting as few in the organization as possible. You have to anticipate the negatives and be ready for them. Unfortunately, the fast pace required is the primary reason that approximately 10 to 20 percent of any story is wrong. The furious nature of some complicated stories can result in inevitable honest mistakes.

Mistakes

You and the media will make every effort to get the story right, yet some facts are always wrong. You are obligated to correct mistakes that have a direct bearing on the story. Members of the media are obligated to do the same. Still, mistakes do happen.

Speaking of mistakes, I once had a very busy media day with two spokespeople absent. I had what I thought was a very simple request from the Washington Post about criminals on our sex offender registry. I made a quick call to our technical experts, obtained the necessary information and conveyed it. I had some suspicion regarding the accuracy of the answers, but I was very busy and decided not to challenge the expert. The Post reporter called later that day to say that there were inconsistencies with the information I provided. It turned out she was correct. I gave her incorrect data. She could have blasted me and embarrassed my organization by placing the issue in print. I apologized, told her about the absences, and apologized again. Because I knew the reporter and had some credibility with her, she completely dropped the issue. I received fairness because I give fairness. Whenever I'm discussing the media, I try to remember her graciousness.

Off-the-Record Interviews

Off-the-record conversations are the lifeblood of interactions between spokespeople and the media. But throughout my career, I have read documents or attended courses warning me not to engage in these exchanges. "If you do not want it to appear on the front page of tomorrow's newspaper, then you should not use off-the-record conversations," they suggest. I had an editor for a major newspaper tell me that he forbids his employees from engaging in this practice. Oh, if he only knew how often his employees disregarded his direction.

I understand why some have great apprehension regarding the use of off-the-record conversations. First and foremost, the term has no specific meaning. You can go to Wikipedia (http://en.wikipedia.org/wiki/Source_%28journalism%29) or any journalism source for a breakdown of terms, but they are essentially meaningless. Whether you decide to use off-the-record conversations or not depends on two factors: whether you trust the reporter you are talking to and whether both of you have agreed to what the term means.

To me, an off-the-record conversation means that reporters can use the information offered as part of building blocks to form a hypothesis. It means they can use the information I offer to create their own conclusions without attributing the source to me.

Some documents suggest that information provided during off-the-record conversations cannot be used in the article or report; it's for background use only. That's silly. If I'm providing information, I'm doing it specifically to influence the reporter and the story. I want the information to be considered or used. There is no sense in providing information if someone's ethics prohibit its use. This is especially true during breaking stories where reporters are rushing to conclusions.

Regardless of the circumstances, if there is breaking news for the wrong reasons, it's in everyone's best interest to correct the misperception before the story embarrasses everyone. No one wants to say that the Governor or CEO is misinformed for the record, so do it off-the-record. Yes, I understand the sensitivities involved, but no one profits from misinformation regardless of the source.

Because of my rank and position within an organization, a statement made by me may not need collaboration from another source. Generally speaking, it takes multiple sources providing off-the-record information to allow a reporter to offer a public conclusion.

It would be almost impossible for me to do my job without off-the-record conversations. I have never regretted a single conversation. Not once has the use of this strategy backfired. For the most part, I have been able to trust the media. I engage in trusting relationships with the media quickly and easily. All this is much easier if you have an established working relationship with a reporter, but it's also possible to engage in limited trusting relationships with unknown journalists.

If the reporter represents a legitimate news organization that operates on a daily basis and is open to an off-the-record conversation where both the reporter and the person being interviewed agree to a definition of what off-the-record means, then there is little to discourage it. Most journalists have been taught by or belong to organizations that encourage or demand a code of conduct that protects sources and encourages the responsible use of the information. A majority of news managers understand the necessity of protecting sources and information. There is a code of honor among many journalists. Generally speaking, off-the-record conversations are an accepted part of reporting. Editors at public forums may say that they are discouraged, but they are stretching the truth. Some in top management may officially disapprove them, but most reporters engage in the practice.

I do not engage in off-the-record conversations with journalists from weekly or community newspapers, cable outlets (that do not offer news on a daily basis), unknown talk show hosts, freelance reporters, podcasters, or bloggers who do not subscribe to a written code of journalistic ethics.

With new and untested reporters, I will use off-the-record conversations slowly and carefully. With out-of-town reporters, I will use these discussions sparingly. With the nationals, I don't use them at all with the exception of newspapers or electronics with exceptional journalistic standards or with referrals from verified trusted sources. With reporters with whom I have established a long and fruitful relationship, my off-the-record conversations are wide ranging.

Benefits

Within the off-the-record conversation, I can form my thoughts. I can run "trial balloons." I can use this give-and-take process to establish a variety of defenses, take stock of the reporter's knowledge, establish who (not by name) is talking to the media, how many people are talking, their level of knowledge, the documents they are providing, what the reporter and editors are thinking, and many other factors.

Reporters and spokespeople sometimes see themselves as partners in the process of figuring out an event. Their cooperation serves each other's interest. It's a two-way street for intelligence gathering. Remember, your organization is insisting that its version of the truth is correct and the reporter is offering sources that say otherwise. Neither of you "know" for certain who is correct, so it's often in your collective best interest to figure it out for yourselves. In most of these joint explorations, your organization wins because sources always overplay their hands (OK, they lie). It may not stop the story, but it will significantly lessen the effect.

So what does the reporter get? Considering how most stories unfold, not that much. The reporter does get information or context quickly. But many observers would be surprised to learn that the reporter eventually (within a day or two) has access to 90 percent of the information "owned" by the spokesperson. During any significant event, outside spokespeople, employees, connected insiders, available research, or other sources will provide reporters with most of the information they seek. Over the course of the next several days, media will obtain the rest through additional sources. They need me to "clarify" their information, but they will get what they are looking for more often than not. As stated earlier, there comes a point when the spokesperson does not wonder who is talking to the media, but who isn't. These conversations usually happen during big news stories where very little remains a secret. Generally speaking, they do not occur during day-to-day events, but if things get hot, suddenly reporters know more about the issue than you.

Obviously, the spokesperson is not going to gain access to the names of employees or other pertinent information that would lead one to establish their identity. As stated, I have no interest in establishing the identity of employees or detractors. Within the context of a breaking story, what purpose would it serve? I have never asked a media source for this information. Even if I was interested, the reporter would refuse to tell me.

There is always some information that is confidential, and it will remain that way unless made public by insiders. The information I hold back is a result of conversations with investigators, executives, or specialists. This is often done to protect an investigation, legitimate corporate secrets, or to protect the safety of employees. State and federal Freedom of Information Act laws that prohibit the release of certain information (i.e., medical or psychological matters) often affect these issues.

All of this is crucial to understanding why it's very important to release bad news all at once. You do not want to make a one-day story into a two-or three-day event because of continuous leaks. In addition, it greatly enhances your organization's reputation for honesty by getting the negative news out first. The next chapter explores this issue at length.

The Quality of Information

In the final analysis, it's not the information exchanged that is important, but the quality of information. Reporters want to know if their source is accurate. You want the opportunity to refute obviously inaccurate information. Often I will ask to go off-the-record and have a frank conversation without worrying about every word I say. Once all elements are clearly understood, then I will go back on the record and provide the "official" version. I may provide about 1,000 words of off-the-record conversation; yet offer just a few words on the record. This tactic helps me to form the right words within the nuances and complexities of the conversation. There are reports where there are 15 references to "sources say" (that would be me on an off-the-record basis) and one sentence attributed to me stating that, "The spokesperson declined to respond" when asked about protected or investigative issues.

Off-the-record conversations clearly have their place in the exchange of information between reporters and spokespeople. While I'm not quite sure that "occasional" public affairs representatives or those at every level should use off-the-record conversations, full-time spokespersons will find the tactic not only useful but also necessary, especially when explaining context.

Context

Providing context can be more important than the facts of the story. Reporters live and die on context. Context determines whether the story is on the front page, the last page, or even whether the story is printed at all. Context means putting the story into perspective.

If you produce a case of defective widgets and a disgruntled employee brings this "event" to the attention of the media, is it really a story? Well, obviously it's a major story if your widgets are replacement parts for 1,000 heart monitors throughout the country. Your case of defective widgets now becomes a national story with profound public safety implications. But a different scenario involves the fact that an occasional case of defective widgets is normal within your industry, just as its normal for a small percentage of new computers to have issues. There is a multitude of scientifically correct, randomly assigned research conducted by outside agencies that conclusively state that one out of every 1,000 cases of widgets will be defective. After all, in this case, widgets are used as replacement parts for broken soft-drink machines; thus the public safety implications are hardly startling. The disgruntled employee can complain about the defective widgets all he wants, but when the context is properly explained, the story evaporates.

Once again, this is an example of the benefits of a trusting relationship between spokespersons and journalists. The story is only a story if the context makes sense. The only way the context will make sense is when the public affairs professional provides it to a reporter. The reporter must have enough faith and trust in the spokesperson to believe what he or she is told or reads as a result of receiving e-mailed documents. In any agency, context is king.

Let Them Go where They Want

I have always felt like the "wise guy" in the gangster movie when the cops invade their warehouse. "I'm not afraid of you guys," he shouts. "You go where you wanna go, you're not gonna find anything here." I do believe the same principle applies to media relations. "I am not afraid of you guys. Ask any question, I don't care," I snarl.

I'm kidding. I do care about their questions and how long the interview should be. Yes, it is ethical and perfectly honorable to limit the length of the interview (one half to one hour) and the questions they want to ask. For instance, if the reporter came to one of my agency heads for a face-to-face interview seeking information on computer systems, then I think that it's unfair to switch topics to personnel reviews. I'm not going to refuse to answer all questions about personnel reviews, but I (and the agency head) should not feel compelled to do it right there and then.

However, I do not recommend restrictions for most interviews. I tell reporters that we are ethical and honest professionals doing an ethical and honest job. We have nothing to hide. Well, if we have nothing to hide, then why do so many organizations seem so anxious to give the perception that they do have something to hide? I do put restrictions on interviews when I believe that they are reasonable and clearly within the best interest of my organization, but for 90 percent of all encounters with the media, there are no restrictions. There are no rules.

In this business, perception is everything. For the majority of interviews that I conduct or participate in, there are no time restrictions and no limits on questions. Most members of the media tell me that their perception of my operation is one of openness and honesty. This perception gives us a very strong platform upon which to conduct the rest of the interview.

Interestingly, I have found it more likely than not that the reporter will bypass items of importance during the unrestricted interview. Sometimes it seems that too much freedom can be counterproductive for journalists. Keep this in mind when considering limits. Sometimes, framing the conversation produces "clarity of thought" that may not be in your best interest.

Technology

The art of the interview is impossible without the means to communicate. To communicate you need the best possible technology. You need a smartphone with all the bells and whistles: two or three additional long life batteries, a quick recharge system for your vehicle, and the best vehicle antenna. Please insist on a hands-free phone for your car. Loading audio and video (recorded on your smartphone or tablet) to your Web or social media site remotely can be immensely helpful. Have software that allows you to edit. Have a portable bandwidth provider (a hotspot).

Note that during times of major emergencies, the cell system will often be down due to too many people trying to make calls at the same time. You should not and cannot depend upon cellular phones during an emergency unless you are issued credentials allowing you to bypass all other cell traffic (as I have for my current position).

Laptops are also must have devices for communicating on the go. Having the ability to change or add to your website or social media sites from the field can allow you to communicate with large audiences effectively. Equally important is the ability to create and edit audio and video. Get extra batteries if your device allows. Note that while you can do all of the above on a smartphone or tablet, having real communicating power and a good size screen can make a considerable difference.

The next item you need to purchase is a hard-wired telephone installed in your home with a hold button and recording capacity. People sometimes expect you to answer your cell phone immediately. A hard-wired telephone allows you to direct media, customers, or other stakeholders to another phone that you do not have to answer immediately. They feel connected, and you get a bit of a barrier. It also allows audio clarity when doing radio or television interviews from your home. Smartphones seem to offer terrible audio quality at times. Employees and others believe that they have direct contact with you after hours, and a hard-wired telephone could play a significant role in keeping them from going to the media.

How would you function if cellular or other telephone service suddenly disappeared? Invest in high-quality walkie-talkies or car-mounted two-way radios. Having high-quality walkie-talkies with backup batteries or car radios may be your sole form of communication during snowstorms or other emergencies that cripple cellular sites and telephone transmission wires.

You are only as effective as your ability to access and communicate. Lose that ability, and you suddenly become worthless.

Media Hell

Momma warned you that there would be days like this. We have already discussed the unanticipated negative interview and have suggested that panic is not in your best interest because many of these stories will lose the effect they supposedly had in the beginning. However, there will be times when panic or something like it can be a realistic response.

I have simultaneously dealt with multiple breaking and negative stories in one day. Sometimes these negative days extend into weeks or months. Usually I don't have to tell my wife or children that I'm having an outrageous day or week. They could easily tell by my mood and my insatiable desire for sleep. There are times when it gets that bad.

So your daily intake goes from five-to-ten media calls a day to 30 or 50 inquiries. Senior executives see more of you than their own spouse and children. Everybody gets very testy. You end up getting a ton of unsolicited and rather bad advice from friendly co-workers, but you cannot get return telephone calls from technical specialists who hold vital information. The issue becomes survival. How are you going to do your job ethically and honestly when it becomes impossible to handle the load? Here are a few tips.

Everything else needs to be removed from your job, and it needs to happen now. Everything that can be jettisoned or postponed must occur immediately.

In quieter times, you will do your own detective work to find out what happened. You ordinarily do not go to your top executives unless you have problems. Now the role is reversed. Go to your top executives immediately and tell them what you need to know and when you need to know it. Let them make the arrangements for access to information and documentation.

Your usual friendly persona may have to be discarded in favor of being more direct with the media and those around you. I once hung up on a wire reporter who called my home at five-thirty in the morning. He told me he was up and wondered why I wasn't. There are times when you have to play the part of a very annoyed spokesperson. But please be careful, sometimes a little levity during rough times will save your sanity.

If you ever needed an excuse to be good to yourself, this is it. I drink all the coffee I want. I eat all the ice cream I want. Regrettably, I smoke all the cigars I desire. I sleep as much as I want to. I tell my spouse and my kids that our lives are temporarily on hold. I put myself first because I have no choice but to do so.

When you are doing 20 to 30 interviews a day, it becomes easy to make mistakes. Remind media that you are under a tremendous amount of stress and all concerned need to double check what is being discussed.

When you have a multitude of media calling the office, you have to take them all on a first-come first-served served basis. This means that the incredibly pushy reporter who ends up being thirteenth on your list stays at number thirteen, regardless of how many times he or she calls or complains. I'm not suggesting that the circumstance dictate turning your back on your friends in the media. However, the volume of media requests is so large as to dictate an orderly flow of responses. Your staff (or others) must promise that you will return calls as soon as possible and that you will make every effort to meet deadlines.

When you do have something to release, give it to the Associated Press or other wire services first. You can call them; it doesn't have to be written. Doing this will ensure that the majority of media will have the story at the same time. This will not stop them from their continued calls; their editors are demanding something unique and will refuse to take the wire story in its entirety without being customized to some degree for their purposes. Also, please remember that a growing number of media sources no longer use the Associated Press and you will still have to try to meet their deadlines.

You are obligated to stay in the office and answer every media call before you go home for the night. Do not try to handle the initial volume of calls from home unless you live alone. You need to be in control of your environment.

You are not obligated to do on-camera interviews on the first day of a big story. Reporters routinely swear that all they need is five minutes of your time. Well, five minutes easily escalates into 30. In the same amount of time, you could have handled five additional reporters via the telephone. When all hell is breaking loose, you can duck initial on-camera interviews. This will be very hard to do, but sometimes it's necessary.

Please do all interviews yourself. Please do not succumb to the temptation of letting others help you with your load. The greater the number of spokespeople, the greater the chances for honest mistakes. While it's extremely difficult, it's best if the senior spokesperson handles the truly difficult events.

We all know that there are two kinds of time: regular and media. As far as the media are concerned, getting an early start on the day means initiating affairs at one or two o'clock in the afternoon. This means that they will keep you busy until midnight. While staying late is fine with me, it also means that I will report to work anywhere between nine and ten o'clock in the morning (or later). I do try, however, to make sure that the television and radio stations have sufficient information for their morning shows to make sure I get eight hours of uninterrupted sleep. I turn off the home and cell phones. Those who need to have instant access to me have my unlisted personal number.

Because you're in the news for days or weeks at a time, friends, associates, relatives and co-workers will call or stop by to "chat" about the situation. Please instruct your staff to make sure that Uncle Charlie and Aunt Mary do not reach you. Others in your office will stop by and give advice; have staff intervene with reminders that you have an enormous number of calls waiting. Interestingly enough, this will not persuade them from leaving your office, but it will decrease the amount of time that they will take.

Accepting Responsibility

I have a childhood friend whom I had not seen in years. We ran into each other at a carnival at the church and school that I attended years ago. After the initial exchange of pleasantries regarding our parents, homes, and lives in general, he said that even though he was not in direct contact with me, he knew what I did for living. He told me that I was a professional apologist. "You know, the same kind of guys that they have in Japan. Every time a corporation screws up, they send out the professional apologist." Well, that's not exactly the reception I had in mind. I try to see myself as a member of the senior staff of an important bureaucracy. Leave it to friends to strip away every ounce of deception. But maybe the term of apologist is not so difficult to embrace.

Organizations are going to make mistakes. Bureaucracies under the best of circumstances are going to find themselves as the recipients of negative news. But many organizations find it impossible to embrace their problems. Regardless of the circumstances, they believe they have done the best possible job and have no need to accept responsibility. I believe that this philosophy is terribly wrong. I believe that the public expects bureaucrats to admit fault or at least partial responsibility for the difficulties they face. The buck has to stop somewhere.

Admitting at least a partial fault very quickly clears the air for both the media and the public. Accepting responsibility should be an act of sincerity on the part of the organization coupled with plans about how the bureaucracy intends tends to fix the problem. Admitting problems is often the first step in the resolution of the issue. Not accepting responsibility is often the first step to problems.

Making News Decisions

What truly drives spokespeople crazy is when bureaucrats or those from the home office declare that the media inquiry does not fit their definition of news. I have an announcement for everyone on the receiving end of media inquiries; we do not decide what is news. It does not matter how ridiculous or offbeat the inquiry is. If they define it as news, then it's news.

Some of the strangest and wackiest ideas I have ever seen have been the lead story on the six o'clock news. Issues that I thought would be of little interest to anyone end up on the front page of the local newspaper. You would think that after all these years; I would have a good understanding about what constitutes news. I do not know what focus groups television stations are running or what media-oriented publications suggested the idea, but I am constantly amused at the mundane and offbeat items that are highlighted in the media.

When we are asked to research a story, often those inside the organization will declare, "This is not news." One problem with this declaration is that it serves no one's purpose. It often acts as an excuse for those inside the organization to fuss and fume at the media. The Smoke Blowers begin salivating. The unfortunate part of all this is that the media take their stories seriously, even if we do not. While your technical experts and significant others will rally to your side during times of extreme difficulty, it's hard to convince them to take these softer stories seriously. We do not make news decisions. Regardless of how we view the story, if it's important to them, then it needs due consideration from us.

You Have What They Want

I once witnessed one of our agency heads testifying before the state's General Assembly. She did an extraordinarily good job under very difficult circumstances. When I congratulated her, she reminded me that her job is relatively easy. "I have information, and they want it," she said.

Once again, there is little mystery to parts of this job. You have information that the media wants. They need you as much as you need them. Regardless of how many employees are providing information, they can only ethically use it if you confirm or deny it. Because the media wants what you have, they are willing to treat you ethically and fairly. Most reporters are not anxious to go to war with you. Unless they are from a national news organization and believe they will never deal with you again, they will go out of their way to treat you fairly. Because you have what the media wants, you have an enormous amount of power. If you use that power carefully and justly, you will make friends in the media.

Press Conferences

Most organizations should avoid press or news conferences when possible. In my 14 years with the Department of Public Safety, I did them sparingly. Unless you have a public safety emergency that dictates the immediate release of information, or you want to announce something truly newsworthy, or you're working for a politician, there are few examples of when a press conference meets your needs. There are safer and more effective ways to get your story in front of the public; see upcoming chapter on marketing.

If your goal is to promote a new service of your charity (and it's worth covering) then by all means hold a news conference. But for many of us, even when we have something new to announce, we carry baggage that makes our agency heads and top executives fair game for any question they choose to ask. As stated, when media is in a group, they can develop a pack mentality that can lead to tough and damaging questions.

One of my former agency heads was at an event, and we were fresh in the news. Three television crews surrounded us and asked him for an interview. The agency head was more than willing to answer questions but was short on time. He suggested that he should hold a press conference right then and there. I drew him off to the side and asked that he address them all individually. He said he did not have time for that, and we should begin.

The event was going fine until one of the reporters started asking questions about a similar event that took place earlier. "Didn't you promise the unions that this would not happen again?" asked one of the reporters. Then another chimed in with, "Didn't you ask for enough money in your budget to make sure that events like these would not occur?" The collective questions started to get nasty.

The agency head suddenly looks at me with pleading eyes (by the way, pleading eyes look great on television). I turned to him with palms up-stretched. I conveyed to him through body language that there was nothing I could immediately do to extract him from this situation. He had chosen to throw himself at the mercy of multiple questioners. If one reporter decides to attack, then almost everyone attacks. I let the interview go on for a minute or so before "reminding" the agency head that he had a previous engagement and needed to break off the interview.

If you have the time, the media prefer one-on-one interviews as long as their deadlines are met. For breaking news stories, schedule them at hour intervals. It never happens that cleanly, but it will allow you to manage your time more productively.

Please note that many in public life will call for a news conference when there is no "real" news to promote. A major utility once created an elaborate setting in a public school to promote a sizeable contribution to a local charity. They had a bevy of well-paid public affairs officers working the event. The place was filled with locally prominent people. But in a combined market with ten television stations, three major newspapers and many other potential media, they received one television station camera operator without a reporter. In short, they held a press conference to announce something that was not news. The concept, however, could have been successfully promoted through other methods. I would bet my bottom dollar that a top executive insisted on a news conference against the advice of his public affairs staff.

For those choosing to do news conferences, there are endless pages of existing materials on the subject as well as comprehensive checklists. Some of these materials give the impression that news conferences require a tremendous amount of work to produce the proper setting.

They do not. Ninety percent of the success of a press conference depends on the level of preparation of the person or people doing the speaking. Focus the vast majority of your time and resources on the speaker. As for the setting, it needs to be large enough to hold your anticipated media. Produce a podium, a spokesperson, and a large enough room. That will give you most of what you need. You do not have to worry about lighting or a public address system. Let the media deal with this. A multi-box (a device in which audio lines can be plugged into) is nice to have but not necessary. It means that the podium needs to be large enough to handle five to ten microphones. Handout materials are interesting but not necessary. Hopefully, they are already available on your website and it's simply a matter of altering and printing what you already have. Flags or a seal on the podium are appropriate touches. Having an exit adjacent to the podium so your spokesperson can leave "gracefully" is recommended.

Leave enough space for photographers to roam up front and in the aisles. The line of television tripods will be approximately 10 to 15 feet from the speaker in the center of the room. Remember to set the room for the media, not a seated audience.

All I am saying is that you need to have your priorities in place. I have seen spokespeople spend a tremendous amount of unnecessary time developing fact sheets that no one reads and worrying about the setting of the room, completely forgetting that it's the preparation of your speaker that needs the majority of your time.

What to Wear

Fashion is another subject that gets way too much attention from media trainers. First, I would like to categorically state that what I know about fashion you could fit on the head of a pin. I have attended training courses addressing the subject and have read materials that devote many pages on dressing for media interviews. My advice: men should wear business suits; women should also wear either a business suit or a suitable conservative dress. Please go easy on the jewelry.

I assume that all of us have reached a certain level of professional competency that includes dressing properly for work. It does not have to be any more complicated than that. For anyone needing more specific advice, I have a simple solution; watch the next White House or State Department press conference on C-SPAN television. Emulate what you see. You cannot go wrong with a blue suit, white shirt, and red tie or its female counterpart.

Be professional in your appearance, but at the same time it is very important for you to feel comfortable. If you want to wear your lucky tie or piece of jewelry (within reason) then by all means wear it. Let the camera operator adjust to you rather than you adjusting to them.

Am I the only person who is turned off by people in $800 suits or dresses sporting $200 hairstyles? Much to the consternation of the fashion industry, it seems to me that you are trying to influence people who own suits purchased at a local department store and who paid $15.00 for their last haircut.

I would suggest that separating ourselves so obviously from the very people we're trying to reach is counterproductive. I don't know who spends $800.00 on a suit or dress, but I know it's not the vast majority of the people we're speaking to.

If you wear glasses, please use them during the interview. I find it interesting that there are people who wear glasses throughout the workday but will not wear them during interviews. Once again, the goal is to be comfortable with the process and to eliminate as many distractions as possible. I find the inability to see properly as immensely distracting. Therefore, please wear your glasses if you need them.

Finally, I fully understand that I have ignored the many interview fashion and makeup tips preached by those who advise public affairs professionals. Why? The answer is simple. You do not need them, and they are an unnecessary distraction. The most important point is your comfort level. Worrying about whether or not your nose or forehead is shiny seems like small potatoes when you are dealing with tough issues. Be more concerned about your communication objectives and your deep breathing exercises.

Dressing for Green or Blue Screen Interviews

You may be invited to participate in a blue or green screen interview. With any luck, you are developing this capacity for yourself or your organization. Blue or green screen means that the background on the set (literally a blue or green screen) will be eliminated and a new one imposed by inserting a video, photograph, or graphic. You're talking to someone interviewing you, but the viewer sees the exchange taking place elsewhere.

Dressings for a blue or green screen interview has obvious implications; don't wear anything remotely green or blue. Most studios use green so green or tan articles of clothing are generally forbidden. Stark jewelry can also be a problem. Note that some cameras and lighting set-ups that work for green screen shots have limitations. In this case, you have to dress for the setting.

Talk Radio

I love talk radio. It does not matter whether it's conservative or liberal in nature; it's a blast. Where else can anyone with an opinion get instant access to thousands of people? I have been a guest on many talk shows. In most cases, I have been treated well by the hosts and the callers. I like the format.

However, we need to recognize several things about talk shows. First, they are there to entertain. This is an entertainment medium in the same way stations playing music are entertainment mediums.

Although a host has never mistreated me, I recognize that being there is like crawling into the lion's cage. I'm on their turf, and they expect me to understand the format and be entertaining as well as informative. That means I will do things that I would not ordinarily do, like giving an opinion. I will make it very clear that the opinion is mine, and not that of my organization. But if the host asks me for an opinion, I will give it as long as it pertains to my area of expertise. My observations will be general and acceptable to all. I will not, however, discuss anything outside the responsibilities of my organization. I will not speak for other organizations. I do not talk politics.

Talk radio hosts can be sharks. They can be arrogant and unreasonable. Why are they this way? The answer is simple; it makes them more entertaining. I'm not suggesting that their liberal or conservative views are insincere. But the more outrageous they are, the more people listen. The more people listen, the greater number of advertisers they acquire, and the more money they make for their stations.

Listeners take talk radio very seriously. They embrace the format as an outlet for their own political views. Listeners do not see it as entertainment. They view talk radio as an important "news" source. Thus, if your agency is in the news, it will probably be discussed on talk radio. Your choice is whether or not to participate. Most spokespeople choose not to participate because they believe that the host will attack their organization.

However, it can be in the organization's best interest to participate. In these cases, I try not to contribute by telephone. Instead, I do my best to be in the studio. Sometimes, I will arrive unannounced and take them by surprise. Talk show hosts like the "gustiness" of your unannounced arrival. Participation can, and often does discontinue or lessen attacks on your agency.

Being in the studio is everything. A face-to-face encounter almost always guarantees civility from both the host and callers. Yep, they were blasting you and your organization. But upon your arrival, that almost always changes. I put together a sheet of important facts that deals with the issue at hand.

I go there with an agenda; it is usually something that will be interesting and allow me to have some control. I offer something unknown. I produce new research. I have walked into an interview and offered a monologue of facts and figures, speaking almost nonstop for ten minutes. This is a strategy you should consider for every interview.

I will role-play the interview with another or myself. I will have a sheet of paper to jot notes. I will flatter the host and the callers. Using the caller's name several times creates a feeling of familiarity. I also give out the direct line to reach me at work (no one ever calls).

I expect wild and crazy questions, and I will try to identify with the themes of the callers. I also try to agree with the host wherever possible and compliment him or her on the worthiness of the questions being asked. I will be pleasant at all times and will even poke fun at myself. I will try to be the opposite of what callers expect me to be (a stuffy bureaucrat).

What I just described is basic public relations. I present myself as a knowledgeable, friendly, down-to-earth person who is eager to serve the public. Being in a radio station is like being in someone's home, and I accord them the same respect. Yes, talk radio hosts can be difficult and so can opinionated dinner guests. I treat them both the same, and I have the same degree of success with both. It should be no different with you.

Here, too, nervousness appears. I do my deep breathing exercises. Sometimes I struggle with the first minute or two. If this happens to you, don't panic; this is normal. As long as you are prepared and pleasant, you will do fine.

Final Tips

I have tried to instill a sense that the interview is the art of conversation between two potential adversaries. The interaction does not have to be confrontational or mean-spirited. The best of interviews, even under the most difficult circumstances, are conducted civilly and without rancor. Here are some final tips.

- Please note that symbols can be more important than facts. In a complicated world, we are often overwhelmed by what we face.

Things or issues of symbolic value often "cut through the clutter" and provide the clarity we seek (i.e., an out of context photograph). That "clarity" may be more wrong than right, but it influences people regardless. I do not bring up this point to encourage you to engage in meaningless gestures, but you need to be aware that your detractors may be savvy enough to pack symbols into an issue. If so, do not fall for the bait. Beware of the value of symbols. Do not let yourself be distracted from your communications objectives.

- The media control us to a large degree and there is little you can do about it. There was an article in a national magazine addressing a San Francisco newspaper that decided to write about urban problems. If a park had a broken fence, they would do daily photographs and articles until government fixed the problem. They could do this to anyone. If they choose to target your organization, there is nothing to stop them. We may not like it, but it's true. We need to do what is in our best interest, and we need to do it honestly. However, spokespeople need to understand that the media has immense power, and we need to conduct ourselves accordingly. We win no points by kicking the lion in the teeth.

- One of the best ideas in handling breaking news stories is to put everything in chronological order. It would be nice if the agency involved would do this for you, but you will probably have to do this yourself. Having a running account of what transpired and when will keep you organized and prepared.

- There are differences between large and small market media. What a large market reporter glosses over, a small market reporter sees as front-page news. They will ask a multitude of detailed questions for an event that may not be covered at all elsewhere. Treat them and their questions respectfully; they still have the power to influence other markets.

- There are times where you have nothing new to offer regarding an ongoing story, yet individuals in the electronic media will still ask for interviews. As the news manager for a television station once told me, "We have to fill up air and we need your help to do it." You can stand on principle and refuse, but I would not suggest it. If you can help your associates in the media, and it does no harm, then go ahead and do the interview. You will be coming to them one day also seeking consideration. What goes around comes around.

- We are not supposed to play favorites. We are supposed to treat all members of the media equally. I'm sorry, but not all of them are truly equal. There is obviously a difference between newspapers with a 20,000-person circulation and a major metropolitan daily that will reach hundreds of thousands of people. There is a difference between the local cable outlet that provides an evening news program and a major television station reaching 800,000 homes. During good times when my office is not inundated with calls, everybody is treated equally. But I am abundantly aware that 80 percent of news outlets will look to the other 20 percent for guidance in terms of forming and shaping their stories. The larger media outlets (i.e., newspapers of record) will set the pace for everyone else at the start of the day.

- You are responsible for meeting the legitimate needs of the media. It is your obligation to be fair because you are asking for fairness in return. That means that you must become an advocate for the legitimate needs of the media. Your efforts will endear you to reporters and news managers. These are the very people you will need in times of crisis or marketing. Again, what goes around comes around.

- Interactions between the public affairs representatives and journalists are sometimes based upon favors. What the reporter does for you on Tuesday will be the basis of a request on Thursday. You have the right of refusal as they do. Remember that next time you ask a reporter for a favor.

- It is perfectly fine to turn down the media. I tell the media "no" every day. But when you refuse a request, please explain why. Very sound legal, business, and ethical principles are often involved in your decision. If they are, then they should be offered to the reporter as explanations for the refusal. Never just say "no" without an explanation.

- The media is an extraordinarily competitive business. Try to keep this in mind when dealing with news organizations. As a policy, I honor exclusives even when it is clearly not in our best interest. Exclusives mean that one (and only one) media outlet is conducting an investigation that focuses on your operations. Even though it would be in our best interest to bring other reporters into the story, I feel honor bound to respect the exclusive. We have unwritten rules of engagement that depend on all sides acting honorably and fairly. But I'm also looking for any legitimate opportunity to open the story to other reporters. Detractors will often shop a story around to multiple media outlets until they find a taker. If that happens, the reporter no longer has an exclusive.

- I will try my best not to inform other reporters of a journalist's theories or hypotheses. I will go so far as to not inform reporters within the same news organization. Reporters believe that they make a living through their industriousness, their creativity, their hard work, and their ability to tell a story. They ask for and expect confidentiality for their work. Most public affairs officers will respect that confidentiality.

An interesting aspect to the above bullet is the time we were involved in a major story, and I worked with a reporter from a major metropolitan newspaper. He took a couple days off, and I promised that new developments would be brought to his attention immediately. He would then decide if he would come back to work or ask another reporter to file the story. There were new developments, and, before I could call him, another reporter from the same newspaper called for an update. I gave her new information assuming that she was calling in his place. I also gave an update to a competing newspaper. The new information was not included in the original reporter's paper. It was in the competing paper. His editors raised holy hell with him, and he vigorously complained to me. He accused me of favoring the other newspaper at his expense and took the issue very personally. The only thing that saved me was the fact that the second reporter from his paper had enough sense of honor to say that she had called for an update and that it was reasonable for me to assume that I had fulfilled my obligation to the paper.

I learned a lesson from this experience; make no assumptions. Continue to update the original reporter. Let the reporter make a decision regarding the involvement of peers.

- Television reporters only seem to feel in competition with other television reporters. Newspaper and radio journalists seem to feel the same way. A television reporter does not seem to care if the local newspaper introduces a big story. They will take the story off the wire and proceed to "work" it (introduce a unique aspect) as if it belonged to them all along. But if a competing television station introduces the same story, then look out! You may be accused by the competition for playing favorites. Just be aware that it happens.

- You cannot do this job without taking risks. In fact, everything involved in this profession is a risk. If you choose to do this job, then learn to accept the anxiety of risk-taking behavior. You are paid to make decisions in some of the harshest environments possible. Some of those decisions will work for you and some will not. Obviously, you are also paid to be right most of the time. Hopefully you will have supportive bosses who understand the need for risk-taking and are supportive when a decision does not work.

- Backgrounds are important to the interview. Most television interviews are conducted in conference rooms. Be sure they look appropriate with the proper mix of flags and seals representing your agency. Do print interviews in your office; it's more personal and it shows respect for the reporter.

- Another "background" suggestion involves interviews in your home. Yes, I did say your home. I accept evening and weekend interviews at home, especially during times of bad news. If the television station wants the interview at eight o'clock in the evening, then they are stuck with me at my house. I have never been "slammed" during an interview at home. The other strategy is to go to the television studio or newspaper office. It's harder to knock you when you go to them. Think about it.

- Many of us will occasionally work from our homes when we have sick kids. This includes staying up part of the night with sick little ones (no one told me about this when I got married). Yet the pressures of the job seem to follow you wherever you go. If you cannot avoid the interview, insist on a scheduled time when you "think" that your sweet angel will be asleep. Do not succumb to their time pressures; you're only human, and you can only do so much. If you screw up the quote, no one will give you credit for your circumstances. Protect yourself. The same advice applies to when you're sick. I took a sick day years ago and received no fewer than fifteen work and media-related calls. Schedule a time for interviews when you feel you can safely do them, preferably late in the day. If the media cannot understand your need to compromise on the time, then do not do the interview.

- Pull off to the side of the road to do any cell phone interviews. I do not care how dire the emergency is; an additional ten minutes is not going to change the situation.

- Know your strengths and weaknesses. Know the best time of the day to do your interviews. Focus on what you do well, and stick to it.

- You are not and cannot be a subject matter expert on every aspect of your operation. Leave legal issues to the attorneys, medical concerns to the doctors, and computer crashes to the IT people. Prepare them well. This advice applies to most, but not all situations. As stated, sometimes you must speak for all.

- Do not hamper yourself by doing a news release for every event you encounter. You do not need a media release for most breaking stories. In fact, news releases can be a gigantic pain that add little to nothing to your ability to handle the event. The process of creating a release and the torture of the approval process can rob you of hours of valuable time. Put together some speaking points in bullet form. These are for your use only and not for distribution. For distribution purposes, read it to the Associated Press or another wire service; they will take it verbally over the telephone.

- Most media will not allow you to use them as a response to unflattering news coverage. They will not allow themselves to be "played against" their competition. This is a tactic that is sometimes suggested by superiors. It's a very bad idea and it conveys a negative impression of your media ethics and sense of fairness.

- Another idea that is not only bad, but also dangerous, is an open attack on the media. It's difficult to put all the times we disagree with reporters in context. Regardless of real or perceived transgressions, an attempt to humiliate one or more members of the media publicly will probably backfire. If you employ this tactic, then be absolutely, positively sure of your position and data. Bring in neutral sources and ask them for their opinion. Many executives become so emotionally involved in news stories that they cannot make objective appraisals of their own situation. They see a "mistake" on the part of the reporter, and they announce to the Smoke Blowers that it's time to attack. My advice is that it's rarely (never?) ever time to attack. Media executives will see this as an attempt to impugn their honor. If that happens, then look out, you are in for the ride of your life. Other media will not come to your rescue unless you offer them an ironclad case. Remember that all media work on the basis of a preponderance of evidence as a basis for filing stories. This means that anything less than your possession of a "smoking gun" can be interpreted as an attack on them all.

- If you have an ethical problem with a reporter, then confront him or her or his or her editors. Request a retraction. Offer them the opportunity to explain their position. But they may know more than you think they know. Be very careful.

- Timing is everything. What you do today may have to change tomorrow. National or local news may completely rearrange everything you planned to do. Big events, especially unexpected ones, can change everything! One of the principal attributes of successful spokespeople is the ability to be flexible and react properly to change.

- Take command of the interview. I'm not suggesting arrogance or combativeness. But you have every right to assert yourself professionally. Try to control the tenor and tone of the encounter. This is more often than not accomplished through being friendly, helpful, and knowledgeable. But it's your command of the subject matter that allows for control most of the time.

- Know what the media is saying about your issue. That "friendly" reporter who interviewed you hours ago is now blasting you on the evening news. It's quite possible that the reporter can influence others by his or her reporting. You need to know what they and everyone else are saying. During big events, someone needs to be assigned to the job of monitoring the media.

- There are times when a television station will have an "exclusive" about an issue that you and the organization consider relatively minor. But it's an exclusive nevertheless. The media have a way of beating an exclusive to death through commercials and reports. They will run the same report over and over with minor variations. Depending on the degree of damage being done, I may ignore it and take the hit. Fortunately, this does not happen that often.

- If the television station spends an elaborate amount of time rearranging the room or setting up extensive lighting, then this is an indication that they see the interview as significant. I have walked into the interview setting, saw two or three lighting stands with the room rearranged, and immediately told myself that the interview will be tougher than expected. How they "set the stage" tells you what kind of interview they have in mind.

- Try to find a middle ground in any interview. Try to give them some of what they want. Try to get them to give you what you want. Shoot for the middle most of the time.

- Try to take the "high moral ground" during interviews. Base your responses on themes that serve you and the organization but resonate well with most citizens.

- Think strategically, not emotionally. Do not allow yourself to be baited. Do not get angry. Anger means that you have lost control. Your ego has no standing during an interview.

- I used to say that we should not ask media to put their requests in writing unless there is a very good reason. It makes you seem afraid of the give and take. But I find that an increasing number of my media encounters are happening via e-mail and text. I'm not quite sure where the new format is taking us and what it means, but it requires fewer phone encounters, which has implications for both sides.

- If you are asked to confirm or deny something, and you do not deny, then you automatically confirm it. They may not be able to use the information in the story yet. But as far as they are concerned, it's confirmed.

- Smile "appropriately" during interviews, especially during television interviews. It makes you look in control and unafraid.

Next, we will turn to one of the most important aspects of dealing with bad news—breaking it first. Like the art of the interview, sometimes it's not what you say; it's how you say it.

CHAPTER FOUR: BREAKING BAD NEWS FIRST

Every book on military history emphasizes the need for choosing the time and place of battle. Regardless of your strengths or weaknesses, the ultimate deciding factor in many military engagements boils down to being ready and taking the battle to them.

I believe the same applies to spokespeople and the organizations they are trying to protect. Breaking bad news first can put you in control of difficult circumstances. Rather than waiting for news to leak out and have reporters come to you unannounced and prepared, you can offer the story to them on your terms. But the thought of announcing bad news will often drive you and your superiors crazy.

No one within the organization enjoys the prospect of a public examination of your dirty laundry. Regardless of how successful you are in controlling the story, it is still embarrassing to invite scrutiny of your problems. Not only do you have to be sure of the circumstances, the evidence, and the position of your organization, you have to do all of this within the context of some superiors and technocrats thinking that you have lost your mind. The primary advantage, however, is that you have the time to do your research, format strategy, and find a crucial comfort level.

But It Worked Before

Regardless of the advantages in dealing with the media head-on, many executives and technocrats would rather spend the weekend with their in-laws than be proactively candid in airing bad news. The major reason for this lack of willingness is the fact that the media did not discover previous incidents of negative news. You could provide 50 examples of proactive strategies that worked, but some executives will remember only the times when non-disclosure paid off with no media coverage.

Every spokesperson will offer examples of times when they urged the release of negative news, and executives declined the offer, and the media never discovered the incident. Few believe that it's in their best interest to make the event public, so no one does. The story does not get out. Even if it surfaces months later, it often loses its timeliness. At this point media may decline to run the story, relegate it to inside pages of the newspaper, or thirty seconds of electronic coverage. The executive will remember this as proof that negative incidents are better left unreported.

Winning the War

Your job is to win the war, not every battle. Mistakes made by honorable people doing an honorable job rarely invoke vicious attacks by the media, as long as the organization is forthright in reporting the incident and maps out a strategy of corrective actions. Yes, disclosure will be embarrassing. Depending on the seriousness of the issue, it will invoke several days of adverse news coverage. If the current event follows on the heels of another disparaging issue, the decision to go proactive will be doubly difficult.

In my mind, there is one indisputable fact: The decision not to release negative news proactively causes decision makers to cease interest in preparing for a public response. They will pursue operational remedies to ensure that the incident does not reoccur, but they will lose interest in public preparations. Many seem to believe that preparation equals release, so they don't. This means you're a dead duck if the incident surfaces two weeks later and the media are armed with internal documents, interviews with employees, and research that substantiates your wrongdoings.

It's also obvious that media will be influenced by your lack of candor. Depending on the context of the situation and the degree of risk to the public's safety or stockholder's profits, you and your executives could find yourselves in great peril.

Acting Dishonorably

As far as the media is concerned, you have acted dishonorably. News people and the public often view all mistakes alike.

Suppose the journalist represents a trade publication, and your mistaken policy greatly threatens the holdings of investors. If you try to keep it a secret, then you are going to get clobbered. If your company does not publicly recall defective products that are essential to thousands of heart monitoring devices, then you and your executives will be in for the ride of your lives while facing criminal and civil charges.

This would be a good place to recount the endless examples of corporations, governments, and other organizations that were caught trying to cover-up wrongdoings with disastrous results, but we already know them. Major companies were alleged to have prior knowledge of malfunctioning tires that caused deaths or injuries to hundreds of people. As of this writing, one is barely hanging on to its existence. Politicians have been accused of a wide array of wrongdoings and denied them, only to be skewered over an open fire when they were proven to be purposely deceitful. The public has been shocked to learn that airline crashes involved prior knowledge of inadequate parts or policies. Some of these companies no longer exist.

As I was writing this chapter, one of the largest corporations in America, a major energy trading organization, is in the process of dying due to insider mismanagement. As I edit, a major car manufacturer is charged with knowingly allowing thousands of cars with faulty ignition switches to continue operating without recall. Deaths, injuries and Congressional hearings have occurred. The examples of government or corporate officials who no longer hold their jobs due to failed and unreported policies that threatened the public interest could easily fill the remaining pages of this book.

Consider Carefully

While it is easy to look the other way when a negative incident takes place, it could have a profound influence on your senior staff and the organization you represent. Like all dire warnings, it all depends upon the context, especially with regard to the number of people it affects and the degree of seriousness or threat it poses to public safety.

If at all possible, consider carefully crafted proactive announcements of negative news. Done properly, they can protect your organization and minimize negative coverage. More importantly, being proactive can buy you a considerable amount of credibility with the media and the public. Credibility is like money in the bank; you can draw upon your account in times of need. The trick, however, is to keep a positive balance in your account.

Not all Negative Events Need Publicity

Does every negative occurrence need to be publicized? Of course not. Like anything else in our business, it depends upon context.

Honorable people doing an honorable job have the luxury of picking and choosing events to announce. Within the life of any organization, there are going to be endless examples of minor difficulties. The overwhelming majority of these do not deserve media notification. If, however, the event, product, or policy has safety implications, or greatly imperils stockholder profits, or provides the possibility of significant negative news, then you should consider its release.

Once again, context is king. Research may indicate the potential for problems for a product made by your company. Under the circumstances of preliminary data, few would advocate proactive publicity. The research would have to be replicated, methodologies must be checked, and new and independent investigators must review all.

Examinations take time. All of us are aware of initial data indicating troubling results, only to be proven wrong through review. This is a normal process that most members of the media would understand without inferring a cover-up.

But what if the preliminary research focused on a product used daily by millions of people? What if there was data indicating that aspirin caused strokes rather than prevent them? I would suggest that this is information that needs to be publicized immediately. Although preliminary, the data has obvious public safety implications.

Undoubtedly, the context of new yet negative research would have to be fully explained. But can you imagine the public reaction if the research results were covered up before being publicized by a national newspaper? All I can suggest to you is that duplicity (or even the appearance of deceit) regarding the public's well being can result in massive amounts of negative publicity and jeopardize the jobs of many.

Whether you choose to publicize negatives within your organization depends upon a thorough and brutally honest examination of all aspects of the situation. Beware of the Smoke Blowers. Remember that it is relatively easy for technocrats and mid-level executives to advocate nondisclosure; their jobs may not be in peril if the worst happens. But those of senior staff may be at risk. You need to protect your executives, the organization, and the public's welfare. Sometimes this unfortunate role will fall squarely on your shoulders.

The Lost Inmates

I represented the largest branch of state government in Maryland, as well as the largest criminal justice organization in the state. The state assumed control of the Baltimore City Jail to relieve the city of a significant financial burden.

The Department of Public Safety was the lead agency in the takeover.

Never in my wildest dreams did I ever expect that this change would produce massive media exposure. Upon the assumption of the old city jail (an ancient structure with origins in the early 1800's), we discovered scores of inmates (over 90) being held beyond their legal time. The media dubbed them the "lost inmates" of the city jail. The story went national and international. We were processing up to 50 media inquiries per day.

Considering that the problems belonged to the city of Baltimore, there were no negative implications for my agency or the state. Unfortunately, that would change in time.

When the state took over the jail it decided to erect a state of the art building costing tens of millions of dollars and employing the latest technology adjacent to the old facility. The structure (referred to as Central Booking) was devoted to processing every person arrested in the city of Baltimore, as well as providing additional jail space for those not released after arrest.

The information system that accompanied the new jail was designed to positively identify (through fingerprints) all those arrested to connect them to outstanding warrants for other crimes or with fingerprints left behind at unsolved crime scenes. Their fingerprints were taken and analyzed by computers.

We could immediately identify the suspect via fingerprints instead of waiting weeks or months as it was under previous systems. We thought that this new technology would "apprehend" many criminals that other jurisdictions would have released because most offenders do not carry identification or lie about their names.

Success?

The system turned out to be far more successful than we anticipated. We ended up processing over 20,000 criminals each year for new crimes and warrants beyond those that brought them into booking center. For example, the Baltimore City Police would arrest someone for urinating in public, and upon processing; we would discover that he was wanted for robbery. We would book someone for burglary, and discover that his fingerprints were left behind at an unsolved violent crime scene.

Undoubtedly, you would believe that all of this would produce positive publicity for my organization. You're right. It did up to a point, but after the initial reports of apprehensions and tying them into other crimes, the media came to expect as much. The story became commonplace and lost its luster.

The 20,000 additional arrests, plus increased aggressiveness on the part of the city police resulted in 90,000 bookings per year. We expected to process only 60,000 arrests during the early years of the structure.

We were overwhelmed. We did not have the staff, the space, or the procedures to process 90,000 bookings. We started to make mistakes. We started to release criminals from the building before we were supposed to.

How Many Criminals Can You Mistakenly Release?

Defendants who were supposed to stand trial for serious crimes were improperly discharged. We released the names and descriptions of the erroneously released offenders to the media, as well as the circumstances behind the discharge.

The first two erroneous releases were embarrassing. The third or fourth erroneous release was painful. The fifth, sixth, and seventh mistaken release became dangerous. Those that quickly followed were a nightmare. It seemed as if we were a daily part of media coverage. It became media hell.

We could have blamed the problem on the numbers of people processed and the lack of resources to deal with such a vexing issue. We did point out the irony of an information system designed to serve warrants on offenders working too well. But the bottom line of the issue was the public's safety and how many thought that we were jeopardizing rather than protecting it.

The media and the public can tolerate one, two, or three mistaken releases if quickly corrected. Once you start moving beyond the smaller numbers, the public has the right to a larger examination of your operation. Did you plan carefully enough? Did you ask for sufficient funding? Did you conduct ample research?

In some bad news stories, media coverage shifts from incident to issue. When this happens, the situation becomes dangerous.

Our Strategy

What was our media strategy throughout this sordid series of events? From the beginning of the state's takeover of the city jail and the implementation of the state of the art booking center, we employed a media friendly commissioner of the new Division of Pre-trial Detention and Services. Under the city, a warden who did not have the best relationship with the media ran the old jail. I advised the incoming commissioner that it was vital that he became everything that the old warden was not. Throughout the implementation of a new division the commissioner was accessible, friendly, and constantly cooperative. The media was given unprecedented access. It is no exaggeration when I say that many members of the media felt fond of the new commissioner. "He is honest and he tells it like it is," stated many news people. He also recognized the value of publicizing bad news. The new commissioner gained considerable credibility.

There was a positive account in our credibility bank, which was a good thing, because we were about to make a major withdrawal. We recognized, however, that once the majority of the good will was exhausted, we ran the risk of serious problems.

Regardless of how much it hurt, we publicized every mistaken release. There were those inside (and outside) the organization who were angry at the never-ending flow of negative news.

Return of the Smoke Blowers

Some of those released were small-time lower level offenders who were charged with minor crimes. We or other law enforcement agencies could easily apprehend them. The Smoke Blowers argued that the release of information about these offenders was counterproductive. They insisted that it served no purpose to publicize mistakes when there were no public safety issues.

They were correct to a degree. Some of these offenders were small fish. But I believed that this thinking was dangerous. I argued that we had worked very hard to establish an atmosphere of honesty and openness regarding the new division. Up to this point, news organizations were treating the story fairly. So far, the narrative had not moved from incident to policy issue. So far, journalists accepted the fact that we were partially responsible for our own problems by the large number of warrants served and a new aggressiveness by law enforcement.

But what if our internal detractors were successful in stemming our efforts to release information on "every" mistaken discharge? "Why are you risking the organization with this never ending barrage of negative news," they would ask? "The information about the release of minor criminals does little or nothing to protect the public."

In my opinion, we needed to be as "up front" as possible. With some stories, what you release may not be as important as how it is released. The perception of your agency may be more important than the story itself. How the media sees you and your organization may be as or more important than the information you provide.

For example, let's assume that our detractors were successful in stemming the flow of the story, and we only provided information on "dangerous" offenders mistakenly discharged. Who is going to assume that each and every one of these lower level offenders would not suddenly turn into a dangerous individual? Who is going to guarantee me that our assertion of "minor" criminal will not come back to haunt us? What if an offender who was arrested for possession of drugs, and was erroneously released, goes home and viciously rapes someone? What if "sources" released this information to the media?

Under these circumstances, I would guess that the media would stop providing us with the benefit of the doubt. All it takes is for one journalist to get the ball rolling for all others. As long as we were brutally honest with the media and the public, we assumed that we had a better than even chance of straightforward, objective news coverage.

Simple Honesty

Our media policy never moved beyond simple honesty and accessibility. We gambled on the fact that we were honest people doing an honest job, and we were taking every possible step to correct the problem.

We did every interview. We took every phone call. We took media inside so they could take pictures and get television footage. We gambled that a straightforward approach would keep the issue in its proper context without jeopardizing our leadership and the larger organization.

The gamble paid off. News coverage was fair and accurate. Although they could have gone for the jugular, they did not. It would have been very easy for journalists to beat up on us. They exercised restraint.

Not that I wasn't scared half to death. When we were into our eighth and ninth mistaken release, I spent hours riding through the countryside adjacent to the city wondering when the media would turn. "When are they going to attack," I asked myself? They never did. To this day, I am fully convinced that it was our relationship with the media and an honest, simplistic strategy that save the day.

We decided to break bad news early and often. There were no investigative media reports. There were no surprises from news organizations. As strange as it may sound, we controlled our own negative media. We kept news organizations in the market so busy with our own efforts that there was no need for a brutal examination of policy. We fought every battle at a time and place of our choosing. We admitted fault when it would be easy to blame everything on unanticipated demand. We told everyone what we were doing to end the problem. We were fully prepared for every encounter. We chose not to listen to the Smoke Blowers. We survived an extraordinarily difficult ordeal through sheer simplicity.

Won't Work in My Market

I assume that many readers will suggest that such a policy will not work in their area. "My media are far too cantankerous and unscrupulous for me to employ such an approach," some may assert.

"The author's relationship with media in his market was unique enough to allow him to employ a straightforward approach," others may say. I would suggest otherwise.

The issue of a candid, proactive release of negative news is probably one of the most discussed items of public affairs officials. I think it is safe to say the majority of spokespeople I have talked to believe that this approach works.

Sometimes, unannounced negatives seem to hang over your head forever. You never know when they will surface. It becomes difficult to plan anything without worry that the endeavor will trigger unanticipated revelations. It is even possible that someone could hold the organization hostage by threatening to reveal the information. Sometimes it's simply better to get it done and over with by carefully going public with negative news. I do not believe that the uniqueness of the market is the driving force behind this decision. I believe that this is a sound and fundamental approach to dealing with troublesome issues.

Tips for Proactive Releases

Once the decision to release negative news has been made, everything else becomes a systematic exercise in basic public relations. The primary difference is that you have the luxury of time to develop the necessary tools.

The first thing to do is to thoroughly understand your subject matter. Do whatever is necessary. If this means spending days with lawyers, physicians or technocrats, then do it.

Begin drafting policy statements that will eventually be the heart and soul of your efforts. Ensure that everyone is comfortable with what is being written. Keep it simple, clean, and clear. This will be much harder than it sounds if you are working with technocrats; to them, nothing is simple, they revel in the obscure. Ensure that your words resonate with the average person.

Once your policy statements are in hand, begin drafting a press release. Write the release as a news story. Depending upon the complexity of the issue, this may be the longest news release you have ever written. The length of the release allows you to provide the basic components of the story and important background information. You may choose to address the history of the problem, research issues, regulatory matters, court rulings or anything else that provides context.

I would suggest a twofold media release. The first part should be relatively short and focus on the basics and answer who, what, when, and where questions. Hammer away at your communication objectives. The second should answer "why" related issues. It is crucial to have remedies mapped out but try not to box yourself into a corner by being too specific. Leave some wiggle room. You cannot foresee everything the future holds.

What you're trying to do is to create is a self-contained press release. This document is so complete and so well written and is so easy to read that virtually anyone in the media and public will understand its premise and the actions taken by your organization.

Instead of reacting to a story offered by an investigative print journalist (with his or her negative spin) that all other media feel compelled to follow; you have spread your story evenly among all media in your market. You gave them everything they need to come to their own conclusions, but maximized the potential for fair and respectful coverage.

You may be surprised to find that a considerable number of reporters incorporate much of your media release into their stories. The package is so complete and easy to read that it may not be necessary to come to you immediately for further information.

It is not an exaggeration when I state that some radio news people read my media releases verbatim and that it was the foundation for many newspaper articles. Only television reporters need additional, immediate hand holding because they want on-camera interviews and visuals.

Your Work Is Far from Done

Even though you may have the best news release of your career, your work is far from done. Carefully selected (or created) well-written documents, photos, audio, or video must be placed on the front page of your website. Needless to say, the website address needs to be in your news release.

The idea is to keep news organizations busy with your documentation. If they are designed to meet the needs of the media, then that is where they will stay on day one or possibly even day two. If you're lucky enough to take your detractors by surprise, it may take them an equal amount of time to read your materials and create a response. Media may talk to them (and undoubtedly will) during the first or second day but they may be too disorganized to offer an effective response.

Enjoy yourself. It will be a rare time in your career when you will face an extraordinarily difficult problem and at the same time have all of your ducks in a row. You have consensus, written policy statements, an easy-to-read media release that focuses on your overriding communication objectives, supplemental material and descriptive statistics that provide context attached to the release, and additional documentation (as well as your original release) posted on your website.

Who Speaks?

Are you done? Hardly! Now that you have all of this in place, you need to establish who will take the speaking lead and answer questions. The speaking role often brings a considerable amount of disagreements. Some believe that your top executive should take the lead and respond to the questions. Many will suggest that your executive has no choice but to take the primary speaking role. I would suggest, however, that this tactic provides you very little wiggle room.

Placing your top executive into the fray on day one leaves you with no place else to go. He or she cannot float trial balloons or try to gauge the effectiveness of your written materials or ascertain the mood of the media. After all, this person is the top executive. He's supposed to have all the answers. It's very difficult for him to say he doesn't know but will research the issue and respond later in the day (as you would).

I would suggest that day one and possibly day two responses to media inquiries belong to the senior spokesperson. It's the job of a spokesperson to take the heat. The spokesperson gauges the media's response, ascertains the viability of strategies, and assesses the talking points of your detractors.

Let the most experienced spokesperson report back to senior executives about the progress of the plan. When you feel confident that the situation is reasonably in hand, then suggest access to your top executives. Executives need to be thoroughly briefed on all possible negatives (and their appropriate responses) before taking center stage. Do not let their feigned "overconfidence" impede a candid appraisal. Remember that many directors don't have a clue about the minute details of their organizations.

Everyone who performs a speaking role should be encouraged to speak from the heart as appropriate. It's okay to express anger or frustration or concern as long as the speakers remain in control and offer a plan for the future. Dignity plus concern can have a powerful affect "if" it's sincere.

The only exception to "others" speaking during early stages will be the use of technocrats. Engineers, doctors, lawyers, personnel specialists or other subject matter experts may join the spokesperson on day one or two to add to the comprehensiveness of your response. There are some issues that are too complex for a spokesperson to explain.

Depending upon the degree of negativity or complexity of the subject matter, however, the public affairs representative may decide to be the only spokesperson. As skilled as technocrats may be in their given profession, they can be clumsy in the art of clear and concise communication. Professionals often have a hard time being brief. Brevity may be next to godliness when handling a tough issue. Also, those technocrats may have played roles in the issue at hand. If so, they may be too close to the problem, and a well-placed media question may cause them to be overly defensive. Depending upon the situation, it may be better to leave the media response in the hands of a spokesperson.

Visuals/Social Media

So the written materials are complete. You know who is going to handle media questions during the initial phases of the campaign. Now it's time to focus on your visuals.

Research states that the majority of people get their news from television. The average market will contain three or four television stations (double that in combined or large markets). Television (and possibly radio) journalists will be the primary conduits that allow you to convey news immediately. Thus, preparations for television and radio interviews become a crucial part of your strategy.

The ethics of many television journalists will not allow them to take a pre-prepared video package from your organization (note that this rule seems to be eroding). Either you have to stage an event with appropriate visuals or allow them the opportunity to enter your facilities to take footage. Once again, the idea is to meet the needs of the media in such a way that keeps them busy and out of the hands of your detractors. Note that in today's budget-conscious newsrooms, Google Earth or consumer smartphone video may suffice.

Have your primary communication objectives or descriptive statistics (i.e., pie charts) placed on professionally done poster boards. Ensure that these are behind you when you do your interviews. Post these materials on your social media channels.

Have displays or cutaways of the issue or product you are trying to explain. Make videos or audio available for explanation purposes. Make sure staff are available to monitor social and mainstream media. If you are going to allow access to your facilities, ensure that they look their best and that trained and trusted staff is there to guide them.

No Press Conferences

I am not suggesting a press conference. As previously stated, interested media should be taken one at a time and scheduled appropriately. Your schedules will never work exactly as intended, but that doesn't matter.

The purpose of individual scheduling keeps media from developing a negative pack mentality through a press conference format. Please note, however, that major unanticipated events may not allow you the luxury of taking them one at a time. Sometimes, the situation dictates a press conference.

Time to Release

So you're done. Everything is now in place. Your news release is instantaneously e-mailed or faxed to everyone in your market. For some of us, that could include hundreds of media releases. It must get there by 5:00 a.m. to be available for morning news meetings and drive-time radio. You or carefully selected others are at the ready to take their calls.

Special attention is given to the Associated Press and drive-time television and radio news teams. Call them to ensure that they have your materials.

The rest of the media and the public will first hear of the story as they drive to or get ready for work. With any luck, the initial media response will be as intended. Other news sources will begin to call to arrange interviews and to see your visuals. By noon that day, you will begin to have a preliminary assessment of whether you have accomplished your goals.

By 6:00 p.m. you will know for sure and begin the process of implementing day-two strategies. You will have to make preparations for subsequent days.

Exceptions

Are there exceptions to the above? Sure, there are exceptions to everything in this business. As I have said, everything you do depends on the context of the situation.

For example, you may be aware of a reporter for a major newspaper that you believe will give your issue a fair hearing. I am not suggesting someone who you believe will give you decent treatment as a favor. His or her editor may (and probably will) object. I am suggesting someone known for fair reporting, someone who "slices it right down the middle."

In times of trouble, I go for the older investigative reporter who has an impeccable reputation for fairness. You may feel strongly enough about this individual to place the entire story in their hands. It's tough to put all your eggs in one basket but sometimes it's worth it.

You will have to be aware of competitive issues and the possibility that other newspapers will accuse you of playing favorites. If you have two newspapers of equal strength, however, an exclusive release to one may cause the other to attack.

A Bad News Breakfast

We had a scandalous report about one of our facilities that I wanted to break first for Saturday coverage. I invited a print reporter over to my house on a Friday morning and fixed him breakfast. After his final cup of coffee he stated that he assumed he was there for a reason and, most likely, he was there to receive a negative story about my agency. I handed him the report, told him our remedies and simply asked for our response to be within the first three column inches. I asked for nothing more than fair treatment.

It worked; we got a factual story with our solutions for fixing problems that guided coverage from the rest of the media. Yep, I had to work Saturday to satisfy all others, but it was worth it.

In most cities there is only one morning newspaper, so it's appropriate to give an exclusive. The Associated Press and electronic media expect this story to be broken by the newspaper of record.

Television and Radio Journalists

If you break the story through a newspaper then everything else still needs to be in place. The news release must be in the hands of all others (non-negotiable) after the newspaper files its story Saturday morning so the rest of the media can offer their own reports. That means sending it at 5:00 a.m. The spokesperson has to be available for new inquiries.

Note that newspaper reports will make it to their website around nine in the evening so you need to be prepared to respond to others seeking information. Reporters using Google Alerts or other services for the name of your agency will see it moments after it appears on the newspaper website. They may call.

Respect for the "electronics" is appreciated and prompts fair coverage. In fact, you may want to have additional resources at hand just in case the article written by your handpicked newspaper reporter is more negative than expected.

Preparation applies to your Web and social media sites. Have the report available that you gave to the newspaper reporter. Some may be surprised by the degree of preparation I'm advocating. What I'm suggesting is becoming more common for everyday media affairs.

Gun Rights

One of the agencies within the Department of Public Safety was the Police Training Commission. This organization was tasked with implementing a two-hour firearm safety course for every person purchasing a handgun within the state. The new legislation caused some controversy. Detractors felt that this was yet another obstruction to their constitutional right to own a handgun. I gambled, however, that the vast majority of people would agree that those who purchased a handgun should have access to a brief, one-time course focusing on safety issues. To most people, it was a matter of common sense.

The standard media release was certainly part of our publicity campaign. But user-friendly materials listed on our website heavily supplemented the release. Users coming in the site could easily find the material through a box on the main page. We also offered self-produced television and radio shows on the topic that were sent to participating networks (which got 230 airings each month). We established who would speak and created our visuals before the press release went out. Even though I felt that most citizens would be supportive our efforts, I took no chances and created the best possible scenario to ensure success.

Unanticipated "Minor" Events

But a well-planned and comprehensive campaign is extraordinarily difficult to do on short notice and during times of competing priorities (which seems to include every working day). You could be up to your eyeballs in day-to-day activities and suddenly find that bad news is dumped in your lap. This is how it usually happens.

Sometimes a fellow employee will wait until the last possible minute before advising you that the dam is about to break. If he came to you a month ago you could have found the time to implement a thoughtful strategy.

So on Wednesday afternoon, a mid-level executive decides to tell you that 50 cases of "alleged" improperly manufactured widgets left the factory three weeks ago. I say alleged because engineers are uncertain about whether the widgets are truly defective. The problem may be a matter of sloppy paperwork or inadequate inspection efforts, but it's probably not a true defect.

For the sake of argument, let's say that the widgets, even if defective, do not pose a risk to the public's safety. You and your executives, however, still believe that it is in the organization's best interest to proactively release the news. You have an excellent reputation with the media and the public, and you would rather error on the side of caution. You want to be forthcoming, but at the same time, you're looking for as little publicity as possible. This is not a contradiction.

The solution is to release the news via the Associated Press on Friday afternoon, preferably at 3:00 or 4:00 p.m. By this time in the day, most of the decisions for the 6:00 and 11:00 p.m. television news will be made. This will mean minor television coverage until Saturday.

Saturday is a good day to break bad news because viewers and readers are fewer in number. You also, however, want Saturday newspaper coverage for the same reasons. You want to avoid the

Sunday edition of newspapers because this is the day of their largest readership. Using this strategy may necessitate earlier newspaper notification on Friday (approximately 1:00 to 2:00 p.m.) to ensure that the news desk has sufficient time to develop the story.

The example I provided had its origins in a Wednesday afternoon notification of the public affairs staff. Like most busy people, it's difficult for you, your associates, and your executives to drop everything on your schedule to respond instantaneously. Before releasing this information to the media, you must still, to the best of your ability, be sure about the circumstances. You still create a comprehensive media release (although much shorter than the one described earlier) and ensure the best possible spokespeople and their availability for Friday afternoon and Saturday-Sunday duties.

Notify the Associated Press or other wire services. Place the release on your website with selected existing materials. You will not have time to go much further than that.

Breaking bad news on Friday for evening and Saturday coverage will often be in your best interest, especially if that Saturday falls into a three- or four-day holiday weekend. By the time everyone returns to normalcy your story could be old news.

This strategy works best for issues that are "resolved" and do not involve significant public or product safety implications. Examples include firings of key staff, completed investigations, or audits that have uncovered problems and solutions have been imposed.

Unanticipated "Major" Events

The above scenarios should not and cannot apply to issues that need an almost immediate release of information. If you're notified on a Wednesday afternoon that 50 cases of widgets "probably" have defects, and they are intricate components of medical devices, then you're obligated to release this information Thursday morning.

Use the same level of preparation described above. If it means working throughout the night to prepare, then do it. Pushing this kind of news into the weekend will bring charges of endangering the public. With issues germane to the public's safety, you must be seen as protectors of the greater good rather than bureaucrats trying to save your hides.

Once again, public relations professionals and top executives are responsible for keeping everything within its proper context.

Kill the Lawyers

"The first thing we do, let's kill all lawyers."

—William Shakespeare

Okay, I admit it; I do not hate the lawyers. I must confess that they have pulled me out of jams. Most spokespeople have a love and hate relationship with all technocrats, but it's especially intense with attorneys. Lawyers and others of their ilk only see the world as it pertains to their professions. Obviously, attorneys view everything within the context of the law "as they see it."

If it's cut and dried, I have no problem with obeying the law. If it's their opinion, then I have issues, especially if their judgment stands in the way of good communication.

Endless numbers of times throughout the year, attorneys have reviewed the same questions but have come to different conclusions. It's their opinion, nothing more. The observation could be self-serving. By taking a conservative view of everything, job-related risk is minimized.

The agency or corporation may pursue a policy that average citizens would revolt against, but the lawyer will tell you that everything is fine because it's legal. You and your corporation could march into hell, and everything would be okay with the lawyers as long as your march fits the letter of the law as they interpret it.

The opposite is equally true; attorneys will often provide advice that is essential to the core of your arguments. They will reason that it is their job to be correct and legally precise. This is how they win court decisions and protect the organization. They do not see a need for their writings to fit the reading level of the general public.

Court decisions can be immensely difficult to clarify. Usually I do not try. For the majority of court cases, I leave it to the attorneys to explain what's going on. The issue becomes problematic, however, when it transcends the law and involves the public's sense of safety or larger policy issues. This is when the public affairs officer needs to do the speaking.

The Wicks Decision

In a ruling with consequences unanticipated by any party to the case, the Maryland Court of Appeals (the state's highest court) ruled that an incarcerated criminal could obtain extra good conduct credits even though the prison system sought to deny them because he was a violent criminal.

Inmates earn good conduct credits for obedient behavior thus reducing their sentence by five or ten days a month. Violent offenders can earn a maximum of five days a month, but non-violent criminals can earn ten. Prison officials believe that good conduct credits are necessary for the operation of peaceful institutions.

The offender in question (Wayne Frizzelle Wicks) had two sentences for two separate crimes that overlapped (or ran at the same time): one for a violent crime, and another for a nonviolent crime. Inmates with overlapping sentences are common in any prison system. The state felt that the offender had a combined "term of confinement" (with one beginning and ending date) meaning that the two sentences ran at the same time. The state was willing to give only five good conduct credits a month (which equals five days off his sentence) because of the presence of a violent crime in the term of confinement. The offender's attorneys wanted the state to give his client five good conduct days for the violent portion of his term, but 10 good conduct days for the non-violent part of the sentence.

If you're confused with what I've said so far, then hold onto your hats. The Court of Appeals ruled that the state could not combine two overlapping sentences into one term of confinement, thus reversing many years of interpretation by other courts, the legislature, and the prison system.

The court ruled that under certain conditions, two overlapping sentences (that were previously combined into one) now had to be seen as two distinct and separate sentences with separate beginning and ending dates.

So What?

What this decision did was force the prison system to recalculate the sentences of thousands of criminal offenders. Some individuals who had already been released and were living in the community owed the state additional prison time. Teams of police officers armed with warrants fanned out to recapture them.

Some inmates who were ready to leave prison in a couple days were told that they were to be incarcerated for another six months.

Some inmates who thought they had another six months to serve were told to prepare to leave in a couple days.

So we had three problems:

1. Offenders in the community who needed to be recaptured

2. Offenders who thought they were leaving were actually staying

3. Criminals who thought they were staying were actually leaving (and soon)

Let's see if you could summarize all this in a press release without scaring or confusing the public.

Kill the Lawyers: Continued

Sometimes dealing with the media is a piece of cake compared to the battles with fellow employees. If the lawyers had their way, I would have been one of those wanted on a warrant and put in prison. At a time when it was crucial for staff to harmoniously work together to accomplish a common goal, we were at odds. At first everything was going rather well. We decided very early that this was an event that had an effect on the public's safety that necessitated a proactive release of information. I spent three days sitting with some of the ablest attorneys anywhere while they explained the case and a multitude of others had a direct bearing on the court's decision making process.

After three days of attorney instruction, case law review, charts on the wall, plus other visual aids and lots of notes, I was ready to throw myself off a cliff. The attorneys were patient, friendly, and instructive, but I still had a hard time understanding the premise of their arguments and the endless conflicting nature of previous court decisions. There is nothing more defeating than three days of instruction resulting in confusion, especially when you are the one to explain all of it to the media and the public.

To clear up some of my facts, I began the process of creating an easy-to-read media release. I was determined to be so clear and so concise that a person with a sixth grade reading level could understand my reasoning. This was "law for dummies."

The Attorneys Disagreed

The attorneys strongly disagreed with my summation. They decided to create their own media release. I would submit to you that Oliver Wendell Holmes or any other Supreme Court justice could not read and understand what they wrote.

It contained more legalese than the contract you signed when you purchased your house. They submitted it to my boss, the state's Public Safety Secretary, who was also an attorney. I thought that we were all dead ducks.

I suggested to my boss that it was imperative to speak simply to the public, especially if it was possible that they might feel threatened by the situation at hand. Outrageously complex court decisions that have a perceived or direct effect on personal safety can cause considerable confusion and anger.

Many also felt that we owed consideration to the mothers, fathers, and the children of the affected inmates. Thousands of people were directly affected by the court's decision, and thousands more could be influenced by the publicity.

Now was the time for simplicity, I argued. Even though the lawyers felt strongly that a surgically precise, legally correct media release was called for, I strongly argued for materials and explanations that embraced clear language. In my opinion, anything else caused confusion and endangered the reputation of our organization.

Simplicity

The Secretary of Public Safety opted for simplicity. I provided a media release that was legally correct (in terms of larger themes), but I also added attachments that anyone could understand. I had five pages of release, professionally done display boards that explained the complexity of this and other cases, and the actual court case plus other materials mounted on our website.

I decided to explain the case from the standpoint of the average citizen, not from a tactically correct point of view. A few of our attorneys suggested that some of my minor points were not technically correct. I did not care; I was more concerned with being understood. But as with all proactive releases of complex information, this was just the beginning. There was much more to do before going public.

The website needed attention. We set up a rumor control operation (with a publicized telephone number) and brought in part-time public affairs personnel to staff it.

We ensured that full-time public affairs staff was available. We briefed all those connected to the operation days before release.

We put together press packets. We were ready to fight a public relations battle at a place and time of our choosing. We were successful in being honest with the public while protecting their safety and doing all without creating fear or perceptions of insensitivity to the families of inmates.

Anticipated Problems

All of this unfolded over the course of three weeks. Regardless of how well you prepare, there are going to be problems. Any major story will involve multiple reporters (and opinions) and a variety of news organizations, each with their own slants to pursue. The overwhelming majority of news coverage was fair and accurate. There were stories, however, that focused on human-interest issues.

Many of the offenders who had been released from prison (and were now living law-abiding lives in the community) were picked up on warrants issued by my Department. Some in the media believed that these individuals were sympathetic figures. They decided to focus on the human dilemma of a former inmate living peacefully in the community suddenly surrounded by police officers at his home and dragged off to prison.

The accounts of wives and children who witnessed loved ones taken into custody produced stories that were accurate but reflected unfavorably on the system. We assumed that this (or something like it) was going to happen. It was a public relations problem that we prepared for at the beginning of our campaign. I think that all of us recognize that large bureaucratic entities, whether they belong to government or corporations, are often seen as insensitive to the dilemmas of individuals who are caught in our decisions.

Even though there is great anger and frustration directed towards offenders and the harm they have inflicted upon society, average citizens still expect fair treatment. This expectation also extends to the wives, husbands, and children. So we set up an information line staffed by experts who could give offenders and their families (or anyone) a complete update about what was happening. The majority of callers were wives and mothers of offenders who were trying to make sense of the situation. They seemed satisfied with the information provided.

Symbolic Acts

We did not wish to be seen as stereotypical, insensitive bureaucrats. Sensitivity to everyone is essential to good public relations. If you are going to be proactive with negative news then the exercise involves much more than tactics for media. Any negative news story will have implications for a wide variety of people. How your organization responds to the human challenges created by your news becomes an essential ingredient of how the public will view you during and after the incident. Symbolic yet meaningful acts become very important and could partially define the story.

We need to understand that many individuals mistrust our ability to have a common touch. Some representing organizations forget this point. All of us need to be reminded that we want to be treated with respect and dignity during difficult times. Failure to do so could dramatically sway public opinion.

Meeting the Needs of All Involved

Regardless of the reasons, whether they are moral imperatives or good old-fashioned public relations (known to some as manners) all of us need to strive for decency. Whether the incident is a plane crash, corporate takeover, a defective product that is alleged to have caused injuries, or a complex court decision affecting prison inmates and their families, it is essential to remember that all involve human beings who want to be treated decently. Not doing so is not only insensitive, but it will also convince reporters and the public that you and the organization are dishonorable.

The same philosophy can also be applied to your overall media strategy.

Avoiding press conferences and taking them one at time to avoid a pack mentality can be seen either as a tactic or sensitivity to the needs of the media. The same could be said for virtually anything that I have advocated in this chapter.

Thus, we have our theme for proactively releasing negative news: meeting the needs of all involved. If we are relentless in establishing all parties affected by our decisions, if we are equally accountable for understanding how those parties will be affected, and if we insist upon treatment that the average citizen will see as fair and equitable, then we have succeeded.

There is little mystery to individual aspects of our profession. Whether it's media accessibility to a spokesperson at 10:30 at night or sensitive treatment to those affected by our decisions, it's all a matter of simplicity and common sense.

I fully understand that the advice of attorneys and other technocrats must influence our decisions. I acknowledge that product liability or investigative issues or personnel concerns will affect our public relations strategy. Nevertheless, I still maintain that clarity and respect for both the media and all others is essential to how the world will see us now and in the future.

Journalism: Never Apologizing

The dilemma of handling negative news also applies to the media. Those of you who are old enough to remember Mad Magazine (it's still published today) know the phrase "What? Me worry?" as the philosophical underpinning of its chief "spokesperson," Alfred E. Neuman. His take on life was that negative events were not a cause for concern. Some say that this philosophy applies to the media when they make mistakes.

"Why the Media is Always Right—Being a Journalist Means Never Having to Say You're Sorry," was written by Howard Kurtz, a reporter and media critic for The Washington Post (and later at CNN and Fox News).

What makes Mr. Kurtz's article so interesting is that he offers the same advice to the media that I (and others) advocate. The article covers a variety of examples where the media made mistakes, or had ethical dilemmas in reporting, but were unwilling to come clean and admit their errors.

Mr. Kurtz tells us what we already know, that the media can be just as dysfunctional as any other bureaucracy in dealing with its own bad news. Many within the public relations profession believe that the media displays arrogance when questioned about their own misdeeds.

Kurtz quotes Steven Brill, a media attorney, who states, "The press has a great double standard.... We spend most of the day holding everyone else accountable, and when it comes to holding ourselves accountable, we say 'This is bad for morale.' Most of us are a bunch of hypocrites."

Kurtz continues, "Mistakes are inevitable in a business that processes millions of words and pictures each day. But as difficult as it may be for media types to understand, there are basic rules of damage control that can help stop the bleeding when you've shot yourself in the foot (or elsewhere). The press routinely offers such advice when corporations get into trouble…"

Kurtz then goes on to offer familiar advice to the media:

- "If there's bad news, break it yourself. There's nothing worse than watching helplessly while rival media outlets slice you into little pieces. By getting out in front, you get to dictate the spin on the story and ensure that your explanations are included in everyone's follow-up piece."

- "If you admit to a negative, you get credit for a positive. Eating a healthy serving of crow helps shift the spotlight from the original blunder to your valiant efforts to deal with it. A full confession also removes any taint of a coverup."

- "Don't dribble out the details. The best way to turn a one-day story into a two-week saga is to go the modified-limited-hangout route. Put all the embarrassing facts on the table or others will stoke the scandal by uncovering fresh revelations."

- What makes the media's ethical transgressions harder to swallow is our holier- than-thou attitude towards the rest of the world. Journalists can help repair their tattered image by more frequently uttering those difficult words: We screwed up."

The Catholic Church and the Sex Abuse Scandals

I cannot think of any organization that has done more damage to itself than the Catholic Church and its mishandling of the sex abuse scandals at the turn of the century. The fallout continues today.

There were accusations that priests engaged in sexual contact with minors and others in their care. The charges have touched almost every parish in the country. Individual allegations were made for decades, but it culminated in a firestorm of controversy in the late 1990's through charges that church officials were hiding the true scope of the problem, and reassigned known sex abusers back to parish duties. Some of those reassigned committed similar acts.

Many suggested that higher-ups within the church engaged in a conspiracy to mislead authorities and the public about the true scope of the problem, and the roles they played in protecting priests. Critics suggested that church authorities may be criminally or civilly liable for their actions. The number of multi-million dollar lawsuits seems endless, and threatens the financial stability of the church, endangering many charitable operations. The head of the Catholic Church in Boston resigned over these issues. Other church leaders also resigned.

First, I would like to state that I am a member of the Roman Catholic Church and have been all my life. I have enormous respect for the Church, and endless fond memories of Catholicism and what it has meant to my parents and my family. I have no doubt that the Catholic Church will overcome this scandal and emerge stronger for the experience.

At the same time, I am horrified by acts committed by members of the clergy. I am equally dismayed by the way authorities within Catholicism handled the issue. In my opinion, they seemed more interested in a cover-up than dealing fairly with victims and the issue. I spoke to various reporters who covered the scandals. They told me that representatives of the Church responded dysfunctionality. Church authorities responded to reporter's questions in a heavy-handed and nasty fashion.

"I've had better impressions of corporations caught in a scandal," said one reporter. "They gave every impression of people who were scared to death of the problems before them." Considering the scope of the charges, they had reason to be scared.

Regardless of the severity of the problem, how an organization responds can be just as meaningful as the information (or lack of information) they provide. Reporters were uniformly turned off by the often negative or unresponsive style of Church authorities. "How dare you question me," seemed to be a common description of responses.

Outcome

According to a Gallup Poll released on December 18, 2002:

Catholics are attending church less often this year compared with the previous two years, and are also slightly less likely to say that religion is very important in their lives.... Catholics continue to say that the church hierarchy has done a bad job handling the sex abuse crisis, providing suggested evidence that the observed declined in religiosity among Catholics is a direct result of the sex abuse issue."

Additionally, four out of 10 Catholics now say that they are contributing less money to the Catholic Church because of the scandal.... The average percentage of Catholics who report attending church every week over the last year, 31 percent, was 13 points below the average of 44 percent who reported attending church every week in 2000.

Catholics have also become slightly less likely to say that religion is very important in their daily lives over the past three years, a trend that is particularly evident when Catholic responses are compared with Protestant responses. The gap between the percentage of Catholics and Protestants saying that religion is very important was 13 points in March 2000. It is 21 points today.

As said previously, there are times when incidents turn into issues. It is almost inconceivable that this would happen to the Catholic Church. Catholicism in America and throughout the world has built up a tremendous amount of goodwill. Yes, the Catholic Church has problems beyond the sex abuse scandals. But most believe they make decisions in a morally responsible way.

You may disagree with those decisions, but I would dare say the average citizen and the average reporter would give the church the "moral" benefit of the doubt on most issues. But not this one.

Go for the Jugular

The media decided to go for the jugular. The media decided to attack early and often. There were thousands of articles and editorials detailing the problems of the church.

But it gets a lot worse than that. The collective media decided the Catholic Church was worthy of articles that go beyond the sex abuse scandals. Investigative reporters looked at overall church finances and the role of the laity in church operations.

The church was criticized on a wide array of fronts. Editorial and general cartoonists openly mocked church leadership. The Catholic Church did not get the benefit of the doubt. At that moment, they lost all credibility.

The U.S. Conference of Catholic Bishops issued many apologies and enacted a tough new policy. Priests who molest children will now be removed from the ministry. They will be reported to the police. The Baltimore Sun reported in an editorial on, June 18, 2002 that the church "came to this new position only after considerable brow-beating. It was national shame—not a sense of moral obligation or responsibility to the church's congregants—that inspired last week's action." Newspapers throughout the country essentially said the same thing.

National Shame

It's my opinion that few in the media believed the Catholic Church understood the position that they were in. Many reporters believe the church asked for forgiveness as a strategic move rather than a soulful repentance.

What would have happened if the Catholic Church in America came together and conducted an exhaustive review of the sex abuse problem? What if they had banished their Smoke Blowers and insisted, regardless of the pain and embarrassment, that they were going to tell the truth as a collective whole and take the actions necessary? What would have happened if they decided to fight the battle at a time and place of their own choosing with all necessary materials and research in hand?

More important, what would the public's opinion have been if church leaders "sincerely" begged for forgiveness and laid the entire process, including effective solutions, out for all to see? What would have happened if they answered all reporters' questions respectfully, honestly, and openly?

Had the above happened, the controversy would not have raged to a firestorm pitch for as long as it did. The media and the public, in my opinion, would have given the church the benefit of the doubt. The endless articles focusing on other aspects of church operations would not have appeared.

Yes, it would have been extremely painful and embarrassing. The public, quite naturally, would have been outraged. The articles would have been nasty and provoking, but my guess is the media would not have gone for the jugular. The incident would not have become an issue. The problem would have been effectively resolved. The sincerest of apologies would have been offered. The victims would be embraced. The offending priests prosecuted to the fullest extent of the law. The crisis would have been manageable.

The Catholic Church in America became an example of how not to handle bad news. I, however, remain convinced that the Church will do better and emerge stronger. This is not the first major crisis the Church has faced in 2,000 years, and it won't be the last.

CHAPTER FIVE: THE CARE AND FEEDING OF SPOKESPEOPLE

After several months of discussion, my wife and daughters brought home a puppy to provide company to an older dog. We named her Stormy, after the inclement weather that accompanied her arrival. Along with Stormy, there came a wealth advice from the breeder. Books on understanding and taking care of puppies supplemented this advice. All of this was designed to provide insight into the psychological stages and well being of the new dog. We were admonished that taking care of a puppy required a lot of understanding and love. We came to discover that this endeavor was well documented, and required much from us to ensure that the puppy was both understood and treated well.

There are a lot of resources about the care of dogs but virtually nothing about the care of spokespeople. Anyone coming into this job finds a rather Byzantine set of realities that few are prepared for. This book examines the media interview process, while addressing what works and what doesn't. It's impossible to put the results into context without an examination of how spokespeople are hired and what happens to them as they progress through their jobs.

It is my hope that this chapter will provide a first step in the understanding of and care for those who speak for organizations.

New to the Job

I arrived at the Maryland Department of Public Safety after ten years of speaking to the media for two organizations funded by the Department of Justice. Although my original role was that of a senior information specialist for anti-crime initiatives, I found myself constantly talking to the media.

My position included a wide array of media-related jobs. I was part of the team that introduced and nurtured the "McGruff—Take a Bite Out of Crime" national media campaign (the nation's most successful public service advertising effort). On this team, I was fortunate enough to work with the country's largest advertising agency that handled the pro-bono account for McGruff. There I learned much about advertising and media campaigns. I was responsible for responding to thousands of media inquiries, and I frequently appeared on national television and radio shows. My specialties were criminological research and making data useful and accessible.

I wrote an array of original documents that were designed to make research come alive for the average person. Independent researchers gave my operation and publications high marks. I felt that I was thoroughly qualified to take on any public affairs position, especially one within a criminal justice agency.

Reality Sets In

When I began my Department of Public Safety job, I quickly realized how little I knew about running public affairs for a large and cumbersome bureaucracy in the nation's fourth largest market (and one of the most aggressive).

As Director of Public Information for the state's largest agency, I had to acknowledge that I knew little about managing public relations for this type of agency. Ten years of experience in speaking to the media about criminal justice affairs, along with a lifelong professional investment in the criminal justice system and four college degrees, did not give me the skills necessary to succeed in my new position.

The existing public affairs staff assigned to departmental agencies ranged from cordial to sometimes hostile. These were experienced and cynical professionals who had fought countless battles with their own agencies and the media and survived. They felt that if I accepted the job as director, then I should know more than them. I did not. They understood what I did not: that spending ten years of talking to the media about crime-related research and the McGruff campaign was inadequate preparation for the endless policy disputes, internal disagreements, and a very aggressive corps of media.

The media was no longer that friendly bunch of people who simply wanted to understand the complexities of criminological research or the goals of a talking cartoon dog that gave anti-crime advice. They could be hostile, demanding, and cynical. They wanted their information to be accurate and on time, and they were willing to make you pay a price for failure.

Couldn't Find Answers

I was astounded at how difficult it was to find answers within the bureaucracy. Everyone knew of someone else who was more qualified than themselves to provide the right information. I was also equally dismayed at times by the misinformation that was provided. It was astonishing to receive information from one of our thirteen agency heads only to discover that it was incorrect. When I received a letter from a major newspaper criticizing my ability to provide them with correct answers, I wanted to fire off a letter of my own asking them how I was supposed to magically know when an agency head was giving me bad information.

In going through this baptism by fire, I discovered that some of my public affairs officers offered little to no help. They seemed to say, "We have survived in this rough-and-tumble world without assistance from anyone. We're not about to throw you a lifeline. You are on your own. You need to prove yourself worthy."

Despite all of this, I survived and thrived, and I have the scars to prove it. Now when a new public affairs officer comes to work for my organization, I try my hardest to protect them and to give them time to grow into the job. I try to get them to understand the subtleties and the nuances of our occupation. Through this effort, it's my hope that they will better appreciate the job and be prepared for its complexities. That is the purpose of this chapter: to provide a guide for the care and feeding of public affairs officers.

Understanding Your Spokesperson

When asked to comment on their jobs, most public affairs personnel have difficulty putting their professional lives into perspective. The job is equally described as fun and imaginative, and extraordinarily difficult and stressful at the same time. Most of us enjoy what we do. We're intricately involved in virtually every major initiative within the organization. We get to "sit at the table" and have our voices heard by decision makers.

To be able to speak to the media, you have to have confidence in yourself and your message; it cannot happen any other way. Although there are endless roadblocks to that confidence, when you speak you have to imagine yourself as a superhero regardless of the circumstances.

The job is described by many as the most taxing of our careers. The principle reason is the fact that our organizations move with the speed of a wounded, drugged snail.

Not Made for Speed

Our bureaucracies are not made for speed. Regardless of their nature, whether they are governmental or corporate, a bureaucracy is incapable of quick movement. You are the only one (or one of few) within your organization who must meet quick deadlines daily. The media has little respect for organizations that cannot respond quickly and accurately.

Ninety percent of all media inquiries into my organization are satisfied the same day. The remaining ten percent require research and are answered with the promise of response within a specific time frame. Acquiring the proficiency to respond timely in this way on a regular basis is guaranteed to drive most public affairs people crazy.

The organization is filled with individuals who are given days, weeks, or longer to meet deadlines. A common refrain goes something like this: "Len, I'm not going to let this job kill me. You will have your information as soon as I can get to it. I have other projects that are due today."

When I tell this person that "as soon as I can get to it" is not nearly good enough, and that I have to have the information within an hour or two, it draws an inevitable rebuke:

"Do you really expect me to drop everything that I'm doing just to respond to some nitwit reporter?"

I try to explain that I need this information quickly to allow me the time to run it by others in the organization to see if they are comfortable with its release. My contact will offer a series of irrelevant questions or comments about the reporter and his or her story. They say:

"So what is the reporter writing about?"

"That's not news. Why would anyone want to write about that?"

"The premise of her question is silly as hell and I'm not going to be suckered into responding."

So now we're off and running into a conversation that is a huge waste of time. I say, as politely as I know how, "I'm very sorry that you feel that way, but I have no control over the reporter's questions. I really do need that information in an hour or two so I can run it by the attorneys and the appropriate agency heads before it's released."

Staff will then grumble for another minute or two before finally agreeing to get me the information I need. If the reporter's call came in at 10 a.m., and my contact promises me the information by noon, then it is guaranteed to be delivered late that afternoon. By the time I run it by the attorneys and track down the relevant agency people to get their comments, I am bumping up against the reporter's deadlines.

If you received only one media call a day, then you could probably live with slow responses from staff, but you will more likely receive several media calls a day, possibly making such response aggravating.

Knowing the Organization

Knowing as much as possible about the organization short-circuits the response to many media questions. Knowing common or anticipated questions and responses is vital to efficient public relations.

Nevertheless, it is inevitable that you will have to search for answers to some questions, and the process of finding those answers can be painful. There are loads of people within the organization who mistrust the media. They also see the questions as having the potential to hurt them if the information they provide causes problems, so they're not always eager to cooperate.

Judging the Organization

If you talk to members of the media, they often gauge the organization's response by how quickly it's offered. A question that comes in and at 10 a.m. and is answered by 10:15 indicates the efficiency of the organization and the veracity of the response.

Bureaucracies that have trouble answering basic questions "tell" the media that they are disorganized, afraid, or have something to hide. This dilemma is solved by being honest with the reporter, and at the same time playing to the reporter's preconceived notions of stonewalling bureaucrats.

My response will go something like this:

"Rebecca, I have a bureaucrat (bureaucrat is media-speak for a stonewalling, media-leery official) who is giving me a hard time about providing information to answer your question. He tells me that he has another work deadline that he must meet today, so I will not have an answer for you until five or six o'clock."

Reporters always seem to understand that you're having a hard time getting information from a technocrat, but at the same time they appreciate your willingness to try. "Okay, Leonard," the reporter might say, "I understand that someone in the organization is busy, but I appreciate you trying to meet my deadlines."

If you have established a reputation for meeting the legitimate needs of the media, then this diffuses the reporter's inclination to see late information as flawed information.

Keeping Everyone Happy

The public affairs officer is constantly "doing a dance" to try to keep everybody happy by understanding the nuances of the organization and the media. The problem is that few are willing to understand the same issues.

There is no shortage of people within any organization who dislike the media and who would rather collect garbage than be seen as cooperating with these "vermin of the airwaves." At the same time, the media is loaded with cynical reporters who will read inferences into everything an organization does. You will find that the job of a public affairs officer will qualify you to negotiate peace in the Middle East. Your negotiating skills will become so acute that you will be convinced that you are ready for any challenging assignment involving suspicion among organizations.

Do They Like You?

Someone once said that it is better to be liked than to be respected. Individuals within any bureaucracy tend to feel better about people they like and trust. Unfortunately, you could be the best public affairs officer on the face of the earth and still find yourself distrusted by some within your organization. Come to grips with the fact that important bureaucrats within your organization will never accept your role. They will make every media encounter a harsh reality. You could be an absolute "whiz" at handling multiple media inquiries and saving the organization, but there will always be some people within the bureaucracy who see you as a threat.

Some within the organization know that you have intense conversations with the media that involves a lot of give and take, and bureaucrats are naturally wary of these sessions. They think that these interplays provide you with a tremendous amount of power, and they are wary of your perceived influence.

It's my opinion that people who are well-grounded about who they are and what they do are not threatened. They understand that the interaction is necessary, and they value you for the job you do.

It's also my contention that people who are uncertain about their own abilities will tend to view you suspiciously. It doesn't matter how good you are (that probably makes it worse). They will remain hostile and suspicious in overt or subtle ways.

Seasoned managers understand that every media encounter involves a "dance." They realize that hours are spent in off-the-record conversations providing context and information, but some people will continue to fear what they cannot control.

At Odds with the Organization

To do your job, you will want to know everything. You will be looking at statistics or quizzing technocrats about operations constantly. While most people within the organization will cooperate with your need to know, they are often fearful of the consequences. After talking to hundreds of public affairs officers, I am convinced that there will always be people within any organization who will intentionally set up roadblocks to keep you contained.

I do not believe that fellow employees or administrators do this consciously; but their apprehension is a knee-jerk reaction to their fear of the media, and consequently their trepidation regarding you. So it is important to remember that public affairs officers often feel at odds with the very organization that they are defending and advocating (something that savvy reporters will try to play to their advantage).

There is a considerable turnover in public affairs jobs. Most people who inhabit these positions are nomads who occupy the slot for two or three years before moving on to other positions within the organization or to another public affairs job. Part of the reason for this movement relates to difficulties in dealing with bureaucracies. It can take a toll on you as an individual.

To Get Fairness, You Need to Give It

To be successful means being an advocate for the media when warranted. To get fairness, you need to give it. To be effective means gently forcing people to do things that they do not want to do, such as talking to reporters or meeting their deadlines.

One of the key attributes for a successful spokesperson is to challenge the information that is laid before you. Not only do you challenge information, you also politely confront individuals about their statements.

To be a good public affairs officer is to play the role of an aggressive investigator. You need to put yourself in reporters' shoes and imagine the questions that they would ask. Then you try to ask those questions first. By aggressively seeking information and not settling for easy answers, you can arm yourself with the knowledge and context required to defend your organization successfully.

This can be an impossible task for an insider occupying the public affairs position as a temporary assignment. None of these tactics leads anyone within the organization to think of you as a warm and fuzzy person.

The Care and Feeding of CEOs

The next basic role in the care and feeding of public affairs officers is to understand that there must be a trusting relationship between the spokesperson and the CEO. This can be an unfortunate reality.

A spokesperson can bring an incredible array of skills to the job only to flounder when he or she cannot form a personal bond with the chief executive officer. The spokesperson could have a long-term and very successful relationship with the CEO but struggle mightily under the CEO's replacement.

There are very successful public affairs officers who have spent years on the job and then suddenly leave because of an inability to establish a relationship with a new director. Sometimes, success has little to do with skills or an exemplary work history. At times, the only thing that works is the chemistry between two people.

Experienced spokespeople have been forced from their positions, only to see the organization go up flames because only they were the best at defending and protecting the organization while they were there. There are many executives who quickly discovered that they just got rid of the best people they had to protect them. These executives inherited a new title: unemployed.

Trust

Much of the relationship between spokespeople and CEOs involves trust. I am convinced that a primary reason that I lasted longer than any other director of public information for the state of Maryland (at that time) is because I was lucky enough to work for agency heads who understood the intricacies of public affairs work.

These executives had been in public service for decades and had run large bureaucracies. They understood that there was a certain amount of risk-taking in all interactions with the media, and they knew of the dance that occurs with every media call. They realized that there would be successes as well as failures, and because of that understanding, they were supportive. Because our success greatly outweighed failures, they provided me with a great deal of freedom and trust.

There was a time when I was preparing to do a news conference, and the Secretary of Public Safety asked me how I was going to respond to anticipated questions. I told him that I did not know. I advised him that I would not know what I was going to say until I got out to the podium. "When I get out there, I'll engage in some small talk and read the mood of the audience. Once I know their mood, then I will know how to respond to their questions," I said.

I would submit to you that my boss had a tremendous amount of trust to allow me to answer his question in this way. For anybody who has extensive public affairs experience, you know what I'm talking about.

Sometimes you do not know what you're going to say to questions until you start a news conference or interview. If the audience is hostile and combative, you will look them right in their eyes and give very terse and precise responses. If they are fair and polite, then you return the courtesy with longer answers and context. Knowing which approach to take depends on your instincts.

Control

Most CEOs want control and loyalty. Loyalty is something that you can give, but control is a different matter. To be a successful spokesperson, you must engage in long conversations involving a lot of give and take with reporters and assume that your reputation for honesty and fairness will protect the organization.

The trust factor in successful media relations has more to do with your relationship with a reporter or news organization than your association with your director. Good media relations means that the agency head gives up some control and allows spokespeople the leeway to do what is necessary. This is very difficult for many agency heads to do. There is no simple way to establish this trust. The CEO must be pragmatic enough to rely on someone to handle the media.

When I first came to the Maryland Department of Public Safety, I would have long conversations late at night with the Secretary. He saw enough promise in me to take the time to establish the personal relationship that was necessary for him to give me the freedom to do my job. I in turn worked extraordinarily hard to reward that trust with successful media encounters. The same thing happened with the next Secretary.

The bottom line behind my tenure has been my ability to forge a personal bond with the chief operating officers and their willingness to relinquish control of the media process to me. Regardless of my skills, education, and successes, if I had been unable to form a personal bond, I would have changed jobs years ago.

Personal Survival Skills

There is a point in many of our careers when the job seems impossible. This occupation is so complex and requires so many skills, especially as they relate to understanding disparate human psyches, that you find yourself wondering about your own sanity. There are few people who understand media relations, especially as it pertains to cumbersome bureaucracies.

A lifetime ago when I was a cadet for the Maryland State Police, I was riding with a trooper on patrol when we were dispatched to a very serious automobile accident. It was not only my first fatal accident; it was also my first decapitation.

A husband and wife were riding in his off-duty taxicab after drinking at a bar and were attempting to cross a busy four-lane highway when they were hit broadside by a fast moving tractor-trailer. The impact caused the taxicab to flip over endlessly and land in a grove of trees. When we arrived at this crumpled mass of steel, we could see that the driver, although badly injured, was still breathing. The trooper and I were using crowbars to try to tear away obstructions so we could get to the driver and try to save his life.

As we were moving into the vehicle, the trooper admonished me not to look down. Immediately beneath me was the driver's deceased wife without her head.

Now, it is impossible to tell a nineteen-year-old not to look at something. I glanced below me, saw the woman, noticed that her head was not attached to her body, and immediately began to get sick. The trooper yelled at me. "I told you not look! Leonard, you cannot get sick! Now pull it together and help me!"

Somehow I was able to comply with his demand, and I assisted him in reaching the badly injured driver. It was our plan to stabilize him and wait for medical personnel with the proper equipment to extract him without doing any further damage. We tried our best to save him, but he died before we could get him out of the car.

Although I understood that law enforcement required seeing and experiencing things that most people would shy away from, I was nevertheless troubled by the experience. I tried to talk it over with friends and family only to discover that they had little experience in these matters.

I found that I could not talk to them, and they had little to offer me. I also found that the only people who truly understood my situation were my fellow police officers. Depending solely upon your working peers for advice and counsel has its good and bad points. I was able to find people who instinctively understood my dilemma, and that was very comforting. But at the same time, I felt isolated from other people.

I discovered that my profession was so unique that few outside of law enforcement were willing to understand it. Criminology is filled with articles describing this dilemma and the subculture it induces among police officers. These articles also described the negatives that are associated with this isolation.

As strange as it may seem, I see many similarities between my first job as a police officer and my public affairs career. I have found that very few people understand the job of media relations. I take joy in my gatherings with fellow public affairs professionals so I can share both the thrill and the pain of the job.

Our jobs are so mysterious to outsiders that they have little empathy for what actually occurs. When we try to explain it to others, we realize that it is almost impossible to define. Unfortunately, this (like police work) produces a good deal of isolation. For a job that requires a very good sense of self and the mental toughness to succeed, there are very few people or resources that offer assistance.

Many years ago I discovered that books or courses that addressed the reality of our jobs did not exist, thus the primary reason for this publication. After spending years conversing with other public affairs officers, I would like to offer some collective advice that will help spokespeople stay in top physical and mental form. For example, I play tennis frequently because it gives me a complete break from my day-to-day realities. I do not see tennis as a hobby. I see it as being necessary to my psychological well being. While I consider myself a devoted father who deeply loves and takes time for his children, I will not allow myself to miss my two to three tennis outings each week. Some of this collective wisdom is included in the chart that follows.

Staying in Top Physical and Mental Form: A Diet for Public Affairs Officers:

- Get plenty of sleep. There are times when sleep is your best defense against the anxieties of the day.

- Exercise! You don't need to run a marathon, but even light exercise such as walking will do wonders to clear your head.

- Understand that your psychological well being will be immensely taxed. Having the ability to juggle endless priorities that few seem to understand and appreciate will take its toll. Because of this, there will be many times that you must put your own well being first.

- Eat nutritious meals. You are only as good as what you put into your body.

- Go easy on the alcohol. Better yet, leave it alone.

- Try your best to explain your job to your spouse. Many public affairs professionals complain that explaining the intricacies of their job is difficult to do, so they don't, but you owe it to yourself and your loved ones to be more forthcoming.

- Understand that many people within your organization have little idea about the realities of public affairs work, but most of these people operate without malicious intent. They simply do not understand the realities. Try to be kind.

- Learn to forgive and leave all grudges behind. Focus solely on your future and not on the past. Grudges will eat you alive if you allow them to.

- The best way to deal with disagreeable people in the media and within your organization is through politeness and civility.

- Learn the art of meditation. Practice it frequently.

- Public affairs professionals find themselves out of a job for all the wrong reasons. The best public information officers in the world could suddenly find themselves unemployed due to a lack of trust from senior executives who know little or nothing about the profession. It happens. Life is too short to dwell endlessly upon the negatives.

- Pat yourself on the back frequently. Be your own best friend.

- Realize that mistakes come with the job. Do not internalize mishaps. You are paid to make judgment calls. Sometimes they work and sometimes they don't.

Be aware of "PIO-itus." There are public affairs officers who take the psychological stresses of the job badly and convince themselves that they are God's gift to the organization. This is the first sign of burnout. This is when public affairs officers become dangerous to themselves and the organization. This job requires a good degree of humility, and when you have convinced yourself that you can do no wrong is when you are the most dangerous. If you find yourself in this position, you need to take a vacation and get away from the job.

In the final analysis, most of us like our jobs. You find that public relations work allows you to live life to its fullest. While you're not a policymaker, you find that the job allows you to have significant input into important matters.

For most of us, the ability to "sit at the table" and to be taken seriously as experts is sufficient reward. Many of you enjoy the challenges and take pride in your successes. Public affairs is your chosen profession; this is where you want to be. We just need to do a better job taking care of ourselves.

Speaking of our well being, many spokespeople begin to look at their employers with something less than affection after being hired. The disagreement involves the job that was offered and the realities of your new position. Can't we all just get along?

CHAPTER SIX: THE HIRING PROCESS: DO WE LIE TO PROSPECTIVE CANDIDATES?

The care and feeding of public affairs officers involves attention to the more brutalizing aspects of the job. Some spokespeople become exhausted by their positions.

Many people outside the profession view spokespeople as good public speakers or excellent writers, while never acknowledging that their principal skills are in negotiations and investigations. They are also excellent librarians, as they're constantly seeking additional data and storing it appropriately. Good public affairs officers (like good reporters) have an insatiable curiosity about how things work.

Spokespeople are excellent speed-readers as well. They know how to take a mound of material and find the information they need in a minimum amount of time. They are aggressive individuals with a good sense of self who are able to withstand the realities of working within cumbersome bureaucracies. The best public affairs professionals respect the role of the media and have an appreciation for the day-to-day realities of reporters.

Despite all of this, when we hire public affairs professionals, we never ask them about their skills beyond their abilities to respond to questions and to write proficiently. All of the above attributes are routinely ignored during the interview process, as few people who are responsible for hiring spokespeople understand what makes a truly good public affairs officer.

A crucial ingredient in understanding public affairs officers is that they are often hired under false pretenses. Subsequently, when they find themselves blasted by both the media and their own organization for not adequately responding to a situation, they are confused and somewhat and angered by the lack of candor of those around them. They suddenly find themselves in need of skills and attributes that no one discussed with them previously.

"No one told me that I would have to be part magician and part psychic to do this job," lamented spokespeople throughout the years.

"If no one gives me the information I ask for, if they feed me bull crap, or if the hierarchy views me suspiciously, then I do not feel responsible for the outcome," many public affairs officers will exclaim.

"I am only as good as the information provided," some will say.

When they are advised that the job requires the ability to obtain information quickly, and at the same time view their superior's comments cautiously, many new spokespeople believe that such provisions are unreasonable.

They believe that it is the organization's job to provide information and the proper context without requiring them to play the role of investigator or lead skeptic. If they do "challenge" the answers they get from management, then it's possible that both could end up viewing the other with a degree of mistrust.

If a media interview goes badly because of the "quality" of information, then both sides may point fingers at the other for the result. This is but one of many examples of common misunderstandings between spokespersons and management.

What the Job Really Requires

If there were a "truth in advertising" clause in the hiring of public affairs officers, bureaucracies everywhere would be sued daily. To ensure that future spokespeople are hired on a truthful basis, I offer the following checklists for media relations, marketing, organizational skills, and interpersonal skills that outline the "real" qualifications for the job.

Media Relations

The applicant needs to:

- Understand that your job is to win the war, not every battle. Think in terms of the long run.

- Acknowledge that many people within the organization will never accept the concept of a long-term outlook for communications, but it must be your principal strategy.

- See media relations as improving over a period of years. Rome was not built in a day.

- Acknowledge that many individuals within your organization want immediate results. You must be willing to live and even thrive amid this contradiction.

- Have the ability to speak to the media and convey the organization's position honestly and accurately.

- Build a reputation for fairness, accuracy, and accessibility with the media.

- Create a reputation that is strong enough to deny an accusation and have that denial cause the news organization to cease interest in the story or to significantly lessen its effect.

- Understand news operations and the realities of being a reporter. You will score additional points if you actually like (or at least respect) the media and reporters.

- Be aware of what the media is saying and writing at all times. It does not matter that this task is impossible. Your peers and supervisors will expect you to know the content of every broadcast and every publication (including social media) in your market. At the very least, you are expected to find this information with the skimpiest of leads.

- Understand that needless confrontations with the media are dysfunctional. An unnecessarily combative attitude is neither desired nor welcomed, regardless of the negative comments of those around you.

- Be willing to fight for the legitimate needs of the news media. This includes advocating their cause even when the story is negative but reasonable.

- Understand that fairness to the media is the best defense against them being unfair to the organization even though insiders will think that you are crazy for doing so.

- Be willing to stay until the job is done. You will routinely be the last person to leave the office.

- Be willing to meet every reasonable media deadline. Weekend and evening calls from the media are part of the job.

- Know how to write and distribute a reactive press release.

- Be on call 24 hours a day, 365 days a year unless excused from duty. But understand that you are never fully excused from duty.

- Understand that there are jerks in the media. This does not give you the right to engage in unproductive combat with them. You are expected to try your best to diffuse the hostility of reporters professionally.

- Know as much about the organization as possible. You are to spend every available unassigned minute in the pursuit of knowledge.

- Assume the reasonable risks that come with the job.

- Engage the proper mix of technical experts and administrators to ensure that you have an understanding of a situation, but you are also expected to make independent decisions when warranted. There will be times when speed is necessary, and technocrats and administrators are unavailable. It's your job to assess a situation and make the proper decision.

- Understand that the media can be unscrupulous and unfair. You are not allowed to generalize these events in a way that paints all media as unscrupulous and unfair.

- Understand that some of your peers will display contempt for the media, and that you cannot allow yourself to be influenced by their negativity. Treat every story and reporter according to his or her own merits.

- Acknowledge that some organizations lie to themselves about situations or breaking news. You cannot be influenced in this way.

- Have the ability to be tactfully but brutally honest in your analysis of any news situation. You are expected to stop your administrators and peers from engaging in foolish behavior.

- Stop your administrators from openly attacking the media, even when they think that they are right. Open attacks invite the harshest of responses and are guaranteed to hurt the organization.

- Be comfortable with off-the-record conversations. You must be at ease with providing reporters with the proper context.

- Demonstrate proficiency in conducting radio or television interviews.

- Be comfortable in a talk radio format. You must have the skills necessary to diffuse an abrasive talk show host or guest.

- Be at ease with and knowledgeable about working with national television and radio news crews. Realize that the "nationals" will not hesitate to burn bridges by openly attacking your organization.

- Know how to conduct yourself in an emergency or during difficult times. You must have the ability to handle a large number of media. You must also have the ability to conduct press conferences under the most difficult of circumstances and create a press release in just minutes.

Marketing

The applicant needs to know/have:

- The fundamentals of advertising.

- How to market the organization.

- How to write and distribute a proactive press release.

- Strong writing skills. You must be able to write and edit with constant interruptions. You will gain additional points if you understand and demonstrate a writing style that is conducive to plain English and successful marketing.

- When to "float" the release to the newspaper of record, thus giving them an exclusive.

- The "interests" of local reporters and be able to pitch the story to those who are interested in the concept.

- When your proactive story is worthy of national coverage. You must have the ability to successfully "pitch" the story to local, national, and trade publications.

- The basics of creating, producing, and hosting radio and television shows and networks. You must know how to market and maintain these networks.

- How to engage in at least one act of marketing each day.

- The basics of sales. You are not allowed to be discouraged by rejection. You must be willing to try again.

- How to implement a marketing campaign with specific messages and measurable goals with a limited budget.

- How to create audio and video, specifically green screen video.

- How to create story-based articles and fact sheets.

- How to set up and operate a website. While technical proficiency is not necessary, you must know how to arrange your site to maximize its effectiveness.

- How to populate your site with materials that are useful. You must be able to track usage and create new features based on this information.

- How to market your website to the media through the placement of specific stories. Hopefully you realize that a negative story that refers to your site may eventually have a positive payoff if your materials are attractive and useful.

- How to operate and engage multiple social media platforms. You need to know the demographics of each platform and the best for your specific needs

- How to create a PowerPoint display.

- How to use a camera, video recorder, audio recorders, and basic editing platforms.

Organizational Skills

The applicant must know or have:

- Excellent administrative and employee supervision skills.

- Exceptional public speaking skills.

- The ability to arrange a press conference and be able to speak during these events.

- Powerful negotiating skills.

- Extraordinary investigative skills.

- The ability to tell when a person is lying to himself or otherwise feeding you misinformation.

- A history of emergency planning and the ability to create appropriate plans.

- How to operate a smartphone and desktop and laptop computers.

- The basics of Web browsers and the Internet as well as a working knowledge of most digital platforms.

- The skills necessary to operate new equipment with minimal or no training.

Interpersonal Skills

The applicant must understand that:

- No one will consistently feed information to you; that is an unrealistic expectation. You need to find what you need on your own.

- There will be an array of fellow employees who think they know media relations. They will provide their advice in the strongest possible terms, and generally speaking, their input will be based on their dislike and fear of the media. You must have the ability to politely listen to their comments while having the fortitude to make your own decisions.

- You're not here to promote yourself. Your primary objective is to promote your leadership and your organization.

- While you may be at the center of many policy-oriented decisions, you're not a policymaker. You must have the ability to distinguish between the two roles.

- This bureaucracy is like any other; it moves at the speed of a wounded, drunken snail. While the media is moving with speed and precision, your organization does not. You must learn sufficient skills to work around this natural barrier and to find information to meet the legitimate needs of the media.

- Some people dislike and distrust the media, and some of those feelings will be transferred to you. There will be people who keep you at arm's length and who will not give you the access or resources you need to do the job properly because you represent something that they mistrust. It's part of your job not to take such a response personally. Understand that this is impossible but nevertheless, expect it.

- There will be times that speed and accuracy are in the organization's best interest. You will be required to insist that technocrats or executives stop what they are doing and focus on your need for information. You may not take their angry rebuttals personally.

- There will be times when superiors will announce their intention to do something stupid. For example, an angry executive declares his intention to publicly chastise the newspaper of record for a negative article that he thinks is unfair. This is obvious insanity. Attacking the veracity of the media is guaranteed to provoke vigorous retaliatory attacks, and it is your job to ensure that your executives do not engage in such behavior. If you have to risk your employment in the process of stopping the attack, then so be it.

- It is your job to convince executives to do things that they do not want to do.

- It is your job to protect executives and fellow employees when they do not want to be protected.

- You must develop a personal bond of trust with the chief operating officer, and you must have the ability to convince him or her to relinquish control over your job in a way that gives you the freedom and flexibility necessary to accomplish your goals. An inability to establish that trust might jeopardize your ability to continue your job.

- You are expected to form a working relationship with all administrators. It does not have to be nearly as personal and trusting as the one you have with your CEO. It simply needs to be respectful and proficient.

- Some individuals within the organization have different agendas from the CEO, and will use media contacts to advance them. You and the CEO will not have knowledge of these contacts.

- Many people within the organization will demand that you discover the names of employees who are talking to the media. This is foolish behavior, and a search will prompt attacks from the media.

- You must have the ability to remain calm in any crisis situation.

- Agency heads and technocrats will occasionally provide you with misinformation without realizing they are doing it. You must have the ability to know when they're feeding you bad information, and you must have the necessary tact to point out these discrepancies and ask for clarification.

- You must be willing to listen to endless complaints about the media and to hear "conversations" about every time they believe that unscrupulous reporters have burned them. You must also do this while at the same time conveying the observation that not all members of the media are scumbags.

- You must dress appropriately for the job and pay for it out of your own pocket. You will always dress as if you are going to appear on television that day.

- You will be asked if you own the digital equipment necessary to do your job and whether you are willing to use this equipment at work.

- They will ask you that question with a straight face.

CHAPTER SEVEN: BUILDING RELATIONSHIPS: MARKETING

"It's your job to make the story come alive."

Up to this point, we've focused on media relations strategies that involve reacting to requests or events and personal survival skills. Now it's time for an entirely different perspective.

In the Introduction I said, "The most important aspect of taking a long-range view is building relationships. We cannot succeed unless we build meaningful and productive interactions with the media and the public. Everything we are and all we can be must be built on trust. I tried to convey the need to create relationships throughout this book, but marketing takes public interactions to a different level.

Marketing may be one of the most important things you can do to keep your organization safe and goal-oriented. Constant self-initiated contact with reporters and the larger community sends a message—we're ready for discussion; we're ready to engage; we're not afraid of our issues.

Media interviews work within the context of knowledge and trust. You cannot do a good job responding to media inquiries if the media know little or nothing about you. To do well, you have to market. Many on the receiving end of constant negative media inquiries are the opposite. They never engage. They never invite the public in for a dialogue. They give the impression that they have something to hide. To survive, news organizations need to see you as honorable people doing an honorable job.

We've discussed in earlier chapters that style is sometimes as important as substance and nowhere is this truer than in marketing. We have exciting tools in websites, content creation, social media platforms, e-mail, and traditional outreach efforts.

In every product I create I have a vision of who I'm talking to; reporters are always part of that mental picture. Having an image about who you're trying to reach is a critical marketing tip.

This Is Confusing

Some will be a bit confused by my contention that marketing is integral to good media relations. Yes, the vast majority of my promotional efforts were done to achieve operational objectives. I didn't market solely to "grease the skids" for better media relations. I promoted the "McGruff-Take a Bite Out of Crime" media campaign because I wanted to save people from criminal victimization, not as a strategy to advance the U.S. Department of Justice.

I took the skills I learned through the McGruff campaign and applied them to statewide efforts to combat burglary, carjacking, criminal offenders with warrants voluntarily turning themselves in to authorities, and auto theft (all with very positive results). I promoted anti-crime summits for two Governors and a Lieutenant Governor. I am currently working on methods to combat handgun violence.

In past and present agencies I've engaged millions of people through social media and self-produced radio and television programs, story-based articles and fact sheets. I want people to understand my agency's and larger issues. I responded to thousands of people through written or verbal conversations about what we do and how we do it. I replied to every inquiry, sometimes spending long nights on the phone to add a needed personal touch. When I volunteer to work with associations and nonprofits, I understand that their missions are essential to promote the well being of our society. I help because I want to contribute.

I also understand that when I'm successful at marketing, I'm creating an environment that makes it easier for people to understand the agencies I represent. The media and public see us as honorable people doing an honorable job. There isn't a reporter in the markets I represent who does not make that connection.

An Interesting Dichotomy

So we have an interesting dichotomy. Spokespeople know how to talk to the media. We know what to do when the chips are down. We know how to handle the Smoke Blowers. We know how to take a hit. We understand that our job is to contain negative news while conveying the fact that we are honorable people doing an honest job.

On the other hand, marketers and those in advertising have an excellent understanding of image. They are experts in establishing rationales to produce the public's acceptance of their products and services. They know how to get people to like you and your organization.

The bottom line is that we have much to teach each other, but we rarely do. Media relations and advertising are two distinct branches of the same field. None of us would ask our pediatricians to treat our elderly parents. Then why do we expect marketers to handle an angry mob of reporters or expect spokespeople to market with the accuracy and efficiency of advertisers?

The advantage, however, is that we can learn from each other. Public affairs specialists can successfully market their organizations with little money if they understand what they're doing and why.

Do You Want Positive Media?

Powerful marketing efforts are possible and doable within the framework of limited time and money. We have to have an honest discussion about the realities of promotions, but I remain committed to the fact that success is achievable.

Bureaucracies are often machines that suck the lifeblood out of every creative person. Lawyers always say no. Finance is always challenging your efforts to spend a small amount of money. Your executives can be clueless about what's achievable. Products are never approved without heartbreaking changes and delays. Completed work sits on the shelf, never to see the light of day.

The ultimate lesson for executives: If you make the process of promotions difficult, clumsy or harsh, staff won't engage. Promotions are risk taking endeavors that cause bureaucrats to pause. Uncertainty and bureaucracies never mix well. Bureaucracies and executives need to be honest with themselves. Do you want or need positive engagement? Then give your public affairs people the chance to be creative and experiment.

In the marketing world, there are few certainties. It calls for ingenuity and an open mind. More importantly it involves leadership being supportive and at times getting the heck out of the way. If not, staff aren't going to engage. Their creative juices will dry up. They will do as little as possible because they don't see how it profits them.

The day before I edited this chapter, I spoke at the Digital Government Institute conference at the Ronald Reagan Building in downtown Washington, D.C. I delivered the exact same message. Staff people were appreciative and said that they were inspired by my remarks. Executives were far less enthusiastic.

We All Complain

Every public affairs official or corporate executive will complain of a lack of positive media. Your new and revolutionary product that engineering has spent years developing produces little coverage. Major policy initiatives that are both innovative and gutsy seem to draw barbs rather than praise. Your organization's significant charitable contribution goes unnoticed. A great human-interest story about your employee produces little attention. All of us can provide endless examples of good stories that seem to go nowhere. After a variety of failed efforts to market the positive side of your organization, some decide that it's not worth the effort.

Marketing is doubly difficult because it's done in the context of a busy organization with a heavy public affairs workload. Sometimes it seems that reactive media or preparation for hard news takes every available minute. At times, the job is so intense and your interaction with top executives so frequent that it's difficult to voluntarily ask for additional duties. Effective marketing is hard work. An aggressive public relations plan can be a real pain to implement.

There Are No Guarantees

I have tried to emphasize the simplicity of many aspects of media relations. The most difficult part of marketing your organization is a willingness to try. The problem is that many in your organization do not see the value in proactive efforts. Many believe that no news is good news. If they agree to proactive efforts, they want guaranteed results.

We all want certainty, but in this business there are no promises. If you proactively market through established news organizations then you assume a certain level of risk.

Whoops

One downfall to marketing is that much that we promote becomes a double-edged sword, which means that some stories can work for or against you.

We invited media to a prison after a series of problems to demonstrate special units as a public relations gesture. Because of its visual nature, television crews and photographers were in attendance. One of the displays involved a K-9 demonstration. Everything was going fine until a large German Shepherd broke free of its handler and ran about 15 feet towards a reporter. An Associated Press photographer saw what was happening and started to raise his camera.

Horrified that the dog was aggressive, the handler ordered him to halt. He did; there was no contact between the dog and his intended meal. The dog sheepishly returned to the side of the correctional officer while I contemplated a photograph that probably would have run worldwide.

Even the best of intentions have a way of backfiring.

They Don't Always Work

I just came from an annual event focusing on women offenders. Women caught up in the criminal justice system have higher rates of substance abuse and mental health problems than male offenders. Seventy percent are mothers. They often have horrendous histories of being sexually and physically abused. Yet they do better than men when they receive access to programs to help them when they return from prison. The event calls attention to the plight of women in the criminal justice system and is used to seek the public's support of our programs and efforts. There's little news but great human interest.

I sent out press releases, created a radio show/audio podcast to support the endeavor and called every reporter in the market and backed up the call with a personalized e-mail. On top of all of this I created a multi-page overview of research on women offenders; I practically wrote the story for them. I used this strategy in the past with great success. Today's efforts failed completely. Not one reporter showed up at the event.

There are times when you use the same formula for promotions and sometimes it works, and sometimes it doesn't. I can supply you with reasons why today's event did not succeed, but that's not the point. Just understand that promotional success is like a relationship where one day they love you, and one day they don't. There are no guaranteed successes in life, love, or promotions.

Update: I am currently going back to targeted media one by one and promoting the same package and theme. It's working. I'm getting the publicity I sought, but it's a slow and tedious process.

The $10,000 Donation

Inviting media into your organization so you can advertise a $10,000 donation to the United Way through employee contributions seems safe enough. You decide to publicize the event but the media declines interest. You take this as proof that all the media cares about is blood and gore and negative news. The organization loses interest in future efforts to bring positive events to the public through the media.

There are a multitude of reasons why efforts to market positive events are unsuccessful. To do it well, the spokespeople will need to be undeterred by a lack of response. They will constantly try, and try again, until they find the right formula to entice news organizations. Those who successfully market organizations are not deterred by failure. They are determined to find the right formulas.

If you spend any time in a newsroom, you will see that every day brings hundreds of press releases from organizations asking for coverage. The overwhelming majority of these appeals fail for a very simple reason; there's not enough time on the evening news and there's not enough print space to cover everybody's events. Those that are successful understand that it takes far more than an invitation to prompt news coverage.

Let's take the $10,000 donation as an example. It is rather naive to believe that television crews are going to show up at your door just because your employees are donating a sum of money to a local charity. In major markets, a $10,000 donation is simply not news (the effort will work better in smaller areas). However, there are ways of making the event interesting enough to cover. Therein lies the rub: Most people within the organization believe that the media should show up for such a community-oriented event. They believe that the mere act of civic mindedness is all that is necessary to gain media coverage. They are naive.

If the organization really wants news coverage of the $10,000 donation then there are ways of doing it. The public affairs officer could search for compelling human interest stories among the employees who did the donating or the collecting. Maybe one of them is involved in his 20th campaign to raise money for the United Way and has collected hundreds of thousands of dollars throughout time. This person may have an endless series of stories about how his donations have greatly aided individuals within the community. Let's also say that this individual has dozens of photographs documenting the positive effect of the organization's donations throughout the years.

The way to market the donation is not through a press release. The best way to proceed is to call or visit your local newspaper or television station and ask for a very brief chat with the assignment or feature's editor. You would pitch the idea as a human-interest story, backed up by an array of old photographs. You could also offer a photographer to follow this employee throughout his workday. I am not suggesting that this idea will work every time. All I'm recommending is that there are a variety of ways to skin a cat. Promotions take imagination and creativity.

Too many organizations rely solely upon a media release as their only invitation to news organizations. In a proceeding chapter, we dealt with the process of preparing for the proactive release of negative news. We reviewed the rather intricate process of preparation. It's no different for the release of positive news. The news release is only one aspect of your efforts.

Giving Them What They Want

The bottom line of any proactive release is to give them what they want and need. Television stations need compelling visuals. Radio stations need sound. Newspapers need news, compelling human interest, or a good visual. They all want good stories. What you pitch to the media needs to have at least one of these elements. Adding several ingredients increases your chances for positive news coverage.

Quite frankly, the $10,000 donation is not the most exciting of events. All media outlets are inundated with this kind of request. Every day, hundreds of poorly conceived media releases flow into newsrooms. A lower-level employee tosses the overwhelming majority of them into the trashcan.

They are poorly written, ill conceived, or do not contain one or several elements articulated above that makes for an interesting story. Community organizations, PTAs, associations, corporations, governments, and many others are all competing for a minuscule amount of news time and space.

Local Media

Even local (smaller market) newspapers that need this event are dismayed by the lack of savvy so many of these authors represent. It's fairly easy to get community news into a community newspaper. Virtually all smaller newspapers will end up giving the story a paragraph or two. But very few promoters will take the extra step of calling the editor to see how they can advance the story to the front page.

The local hospital may want to publicize the fact that it has 15 volunteers who are celebrating their 10th anniversary of service. Instead of relying on a press release, it's probably much better to contact the editor and ask for or suggest a more comprehensive approach. "I have a great idea for the front page," is a gutsy way to start a conversation.

There's not much "news" in the fact that some of your volunteers have long histories of service. But there's probably an endless array of interesting stories connected to these individuals. It's your job to find those interesting stories and pitch them to the local newspaper. It's your job to establish the best photo opportunities. It's your job to make the story come alive.

Make It as Easy as Possible

The best way of getting your story placed is to make the reporter's job as easy as possible. Assignment editors do not like the barrage of requests for coverage, especially when those they receive are boring and do not appeal to their audience. You need to separate yourself from the horde.

Reporters appreciate savvy requestors. They're always on the lookout for news or dynamite photographs, for compelling human-interest stories or interesting sounds. Reporters and editors are constantly searching for these elements. You need to offer them on a silver platter. Your job is to make it as easy as possible for them to cover the story.

If what you have does not contain the essential elements of an interesting story, then do everyone a favor and do not promote it. If you are satisfied with two paragraphs on page four of your community newspaper, then fine. But if you want television or radio or major newspaper coverage, then you have to give them what they need, not what you think they need.

The Most Interesting Person

What makes any event succeed is a little bit of hard news and a lot of human interest and visuals. Work hard to find the most interesting people connected to the story. Sit down and interview them. Find out what makes them interesting. Relay this information to the media.

Strive to find an individual who describes his struggle in terms that the average person can relate to. Find Mr. "Every Man" and Ms. "Every Woman" who describes a story of adversity, and hopefully of success against all odds. This person could be from your engineering department, someone who struggled for years before finding the right formula for a new product. She could be the one who discovered a new way to recycle widgets. Or she may offer an improved method of placing foster children into the homes of loving parents, and at the same time you discover that she, too, was raised in a foster home.

The bottom line behind this advice is to put the most interesting people up front and place your executives in the rear. Some executives may not love you, but the media will, and you will get the story. That will please the chief executive!

As to press conferences, I am not suggesting that important people be ignored. Have the most important people there as the main speakers, be sure that they acknowledge others by name and laud their contributions. Celebrate them. Just don't ask them to speak unless they are primary characters in the story. Even then, ask them to hold their remarks to a minute or two.

One Reporter

Sometimes the best way of publicizing your event is to pitch a truly interesting story to one reporter with hopes of having it picked up by the Associated Press. This means placing it with a major newspaper reporter and giving him or her an exclusive.

You will know whether a reporter is excited about your idea early in the process. With your willingness to throw in compelling visuals and interviews with your leadership, you may find that the best way of distributing your media release is not distributing it at all. Your interested reporter will do the job for you.

The drawback to this strategy is that it may take weeks to employ. Positive information, regardless of how compelling, is generally soft news that may take a back seat to hard news stories. I have waited months for a finished positive story to appear. It was so lengthy that the editors were waiting for a "lull in the action" before running it.

I suggest you give a like-minded reporter the time to develop the story properly. Ending up on the front page of a major newspaper will provide your issue with a ton of positive publicity.

You also have the option (or obligation depending on the circumstances) of running a media release concurrently with the reporter's story. So you have the best of all worlds: a front-page newspaper article plus an Associated Press story and a media release automatically sent to all others in your market. It does not get any better than this.

No Money to Market

Some context: In my world, the majority of public affairs people possess few or limited resources to market. I understand that some reading this book will have reasonable or considerable assets, but most will not. As a consequence, I try to present strategies that are achievable by anyone. All of my successes in promotions had very challenging budgets.

Obviously there has to be "some" money and person power available, but I maintain that you can obtain millions of dollars in marketing while stretching available dollars to their limit. But we cannot do a good job of marketing without a brief understanding of traditional methods of advertising. There are lessons to be learned that apply to us all regardless of budget.

Advertising Agencies: Important Lessons

Major corporations along with a few government organizations (with dedicated funding to promote an issue) spend billions of dollars to systematically promote products, ideas, and themselves while achieving defined goals. Messages are usually defined by action: buy a burger, buy a car, give to the Red Cross, etc. Keep this in mind.

For corporations, marketing means the choice of a competent public relations firm, managing their accounts, and paying for their efforts. General Motors, McDonalds, Google, Apple, and your local hospital or car dealership all live and die on efforts to publicize their products and entice people to spend their money. You may think of Google as a search engine. It's not. It's an advertising platform. The same applies to Facebook and the majority of social media sites. All have to study their data, monetize, or die.

Algorithms employed by every business crunch huge amounts of data that tells organizations (or the National Security Agency) what's happening in their worlds. The numbers are meant to do one thing: create the most effective methods to accomplish their goals.

Developing a Message

Those of us who lack advertising budgets can successfully market. The trick is to understand what we mean by marketing. Corporations who live and die based upon their ability to market establish very tight and precise messages. They understand that the public has a very limited tolerance for unclear messages. Developing that message is an essential ingredient in changing images or convincing a person to take a specific action. Establishing a reputation for quality and value is their ultimate goal. They want to convince you that their product is worthy of your attention. An endless amount of effort will go into producing a brand or slogan that you will remember favorably. They will invest years establishing overriding communication objectives. Marketers will pick measurable messages and hammer away at them relentlessly.

Brevity

What can we learn from this process? Brevity is next to godliness. We need communication objectives that are clean, crisp, and easy to understand that resonate with the general public. The public has limited patience—something that professional advertisers take for granted. Some of our representatives ramble on endlessly. No one seems to have the ability to get to the point.

We bristle at the thought of fact sheets instead of long documents. We rebel at taking complicated court decisions and turning them into one-page submissions that the average person will understand. We use ten pages of explanation when four paragraphs will do just fine. Some of us find it beneath our dignity, education, and standing to communicate with pinpoint accuracy.

But we harm ourselves in the process. We would rather be vague and obscure principally because we're encouraged to be that way. We produce grammatically correct but imprecise press releases because we are taught that tactical writing is an art that marks us as educated human beings.

Me and McGruff

During the "McGruff-Take a Bite Out of Crime" national media campaign I ran two federally funded national information centers on crime prevention and spoke to the media. I supplied crime research and statistics and worked with some of the best in the advertising world. I saw firsthand how effective the marketing and creative communities could be (Saatchie and Saatchie was the pro-bono agency working through the Ad Council). They offered me the chance to learn advertising, and I incorporated those principles into successful shoestring and low-budget media campaigns. I could take small amounts of money and turn it into successful marketing that achieved specific goals because of what I was taught. So can you.

The folks at Saatchie told me that I had to agree to surgically remove the top of my head, extract all prior knowledge of what I thought advertising was and open myself up to the creative process. If I wasn't willing to throw away all preconceived notions of marketing and advertising, and if I could not get in touch with my creative side, there was little sense in teaching me their craft.

Two things became apparent through the McGruff campaign; the professional marketers I worked with were amazingly creative, and we became the nation's most successful public service marketing effort. They were smart, funny, and engaging. They understood what it takes to get people to do something.

All of us wish that we could take advantage of the work of advertising agencies. If we cannot, we can at least keep their methods and objectives in mind. What they do and how they do it contains important lessons for the rest of us. They are simply amazing; we should pay attention.

Knowing How to Advertise

Corporations and a few nonprofits know how to market. Marketing and sales are the lifeblood of their existence. All of these organizations know exactly what they want from their marketing plan and are prepared to pay for it. They purchase the latest demographic and economic research to decide the location of their business or branch office. They understand their local, regional, or national markets. Extensive survey research will be employed to understand their customers better. Focus groups will be used after survey research to fine-tune their messages. Products will be test marketed in certain areas in unique ways to ascertain consumer preferences. They will crunch massive amounts of data and analyze everything. Ever wonder why your store gives you a discount to sign up for their club card? They want to know as much as possible about you, your neighbors, your community and your spending habits.

Advertising agencies will suggest segmented strategies to reach particular groups. Sales executives and marketing specialists will gather with experts from advertising agencies to establish which of a variety of strategies is having the greatest effect. Information will be gathered from individuals purchasing goods and services. Social media efforts will be analyzed. All of this will be well documented with easy-to-read descriptive statistics.

Senior representatives from sales and marketing will gather with their counterparts from the advertising agency and produce an endless array of pie charts and histograms. Their overriding communication objectives and descriptive statistics will be mounted on professionally done poster boards and loaded into an intriguing PowerPoint presentation which will be used to brief senior executives. Millions of dollars will be committed to a specific plan employing precise timetables.

Sales and demographic data will be gathered and analyzed at key points in the campaign to establish progress. The corporation and their marketing experts will be savvy enough to establish what's working and what's not. Changes will be made as necessary; messages will be fine-tuned, and the organization will have the resources to make mid-course corrections. The business will know exactly what it wants to accomplish and will do what is necessary to succeed.

For organizations that live and die with this process, they ensure that it is done properly. Without marketing, without sales, and without understanding their customer base, they cease to exist. Variations on that theme apply equally to us all.

So the Gods of Advertising Rule?

So the gods of advertising rule? Not necessarily. They are very good what they do. We are very good at interacting with the media. The interesting part is that some of the best of corporations, regardless of their marketing expertise, will fold like Nervous Nellies when they find themselves on the receiving end of relentless negative media inquiries. There is a huge difference between marketing, advertising, and media relations.

You can be a whiz at focus groups, or a fantastic and creative writer, but none of this means a hill of beans if you do not know how to talk to reporters. An aggressive, hard-nosed reporter who has done his or her homework is not impressed by the fact that you purchase millions of dollars in advertising. It may make the "chase" that much more interesting.

The tragedy is that all of your efforts and all the money spent to understand and entice customers may completely disappear (along with your company) if the reporter possesses significant negative news and you mishandle the process. All the advertising in the world will not overcome scandalous front-page newspaper articles in media throughout the country.

Marketing: A Clear Understanding

The major difference between you and everyone else is that you have a very clear understanding of what marketing means. You know exactly what you're capable of doing and what's realistic. Your leadership (hopefully) also understands this. You cannot do everything that professional advertisers do because of budget. But you can accomplish your objectives. The rest of this chapter will show you how.

What Professional Marketers Do

Professional marketers are very good at accomplishing the following tasks. They:

- Know how to set precise objectives.

- Will not allow clients to be unrealistic about what they're trying to accomplish.

- Will work within allotted budgets to get the biggest bang for their client's money.

- Understand that there is a huge difference between the public's ability to: (1) recognize the product or person or policy; (2) feel favorably about what is being promoted, and most important of all, (3) take the specified action desired. They know that it might take different methods to accomplish each of these goals.

- Understand that there is a world of difference between a weekend campaign to sell cars in one location and a multi-month effort to establish a favorable image for a national product.

- Know exactly what they want the public to do. They communicate this clearly and succulently. They embrace brevity.

- Study targeted, segmented audiences to ascertain what marketers need to say or do to get the public to take specific actions.

- Find or hire the best people for the job. They know that some individuals are best at understanding the needs of children while others are experts in reaching adults.

- Come to very firm conclusions about the best methods for reaching their intended audience. Options include radio, television, or newspaper ads. Other possibilities include direct mail marketing, telemarketing, billboards, fliers delivered directly to the home, e-mail, Internet ads, social media, or creating events that draw mainstream media or trade publications.

- Will use a variety of techniques at different times and in different ways to accomplish their goals.

- Understand that they may have to "hit" their audience several times in different ways (i.e., TV, radio, social media) within a specific period to be successful. Some preach three times in three ways within one month.

- Will hire the best "creatives." Photographers, writers, and illustrators are all part of the mix. They will hire production companies with competent directors to create effective (often funny) radio and television ads or video press releases. Regardless of the medium, these ads will be interesting, amusing, or visually compelling. They will grab the consumers' interest and make them pay attention.

- Measure their target audiences multiple times to see if their message is effective.

- Understand that multiple midcourse corrections are necessary to fine-tune their message.

- Conduct research on groups that both comply with or ignore their message.

- Study vast data sets bought or collected through legitimate means.

- Produce a variety of easy-to-understand descriptive statistics so that decision makers and funders can make the best possible decisions.

- Come to very firm conclusions about the success or lack of success of efforts and provide options for improving marketing efforts in the future.

- Understand that timing means everything. Successful campaigns during good economic times may change significantly due to economic downturns.

- Will do all of this over and over until they have the right mix of strategies to produce the desired effects.

Understanding Our Limits

Public affairs professionals (and hopefully their executives) are good at understanding the following limitations. They:

- Understand that they are limited in their ability to reach a segmented audience with a specific message. I didn't say it was impossible, just challenging.

- Acknowledge that without money, marketing plans are somewhat useless. Putting it on paper doesn't make it happen. True marketing plans are well-funded entities with the resources to accomplish goals within precise timetables.

- Recognize that they cannot control the flow of media efforts thus they will not be hitting their target audience three times in three different ways during a specific time period.

- Know that they are limited in producing measurable results that indicate progress or lack of progress.

- Understand that marketing is a function that will take place almost entirely in-house. Their research and their creative team will draw from resources at hand or on the Internet. This will be a time consuming process.

- Are successful in advising executives about the limits of marketing with limited resources. Some executives and others can be clueless about the organization's ability to market effectively without a significant infusion of funds. Sometimes, executives need to be "brought back to earth" with regard to what is possible without spending significant sums of money.

- Are very aware that marketing efforts, regardless of how successful they are, are limited in their ability to change public opinion or to get the public to accomplish a specific task. They understand that measurable changes in public attitudes come as a result of sustained advertising efforts. That takes money. Without funds, marketing efforts, regardless of how creative, may be capable of only limited results.

What We Can Do

We can do things that professional marketers cannot do. Public affairs professionals with an aggressive marketing strategy are very good at the following tasks. They:

- Understand that they can get on the front page of major newspapers, often with compelling photographs. My organizations have been on the front page of the Metro section of The Washington Post with a positive story where a third of the page was taken up by verbiage and photographs. This is not unusual.

- Know that they can be a primary story on a television broadcast reaching hundreds of thousands of homes.

- Realize that a good story can receive multiple radio plays on targeted radio stations at the best possible times.

- Are aware that they can do any of the above multiple times, and generate hundreds of thousands if not millions of dollars of positive marketing.

- Fully understand that they can accomplish feats of advertising that professional public relations firms can only dream about. Even the best advertising firms in the world cannot buy access to the front pages of major newspapers or be lead stories on television or radio.

- Know that they and their executives can be regulars on the talk show circuit.

- Are constantly on radio station public affairs shows.

- Know that with donated radio studio time and with a minor expense of copying CDs they can create a radio network and reach audiences throughout their target area.

- Realize that cable access or university television stations will often create shows for a very reasonable cost and distribute them throughout their markets. With my current organization, we get 600 television airings a year. We have over 50,000 views on YouTube. We have had as many as 1.4 million page views on our radio and television website.

- Create their own audio and video programs in-house and place the products on your website or distribute to radio and television stations. I create 30-minute radio programs in my own studio. We are in the process of creating green screen videos to complement the television shows we record in a public access station.

- Have excellent contacts with reporters in their market. They know the interests of news people and editors and pitch stories that will likely get attention.

- Know that the story you pitch does not necessarily have to be "favorable." If media examines an aspect of your operation, and you wind up on the front page of the local newspaper with a story that is neither positive nor negative, then you have won. As strange as it sounds, it does not have to be a positive story to produce a positive result, especially if media connects it to your website and materials you control.

- Develop lists of employees or volunteers that have unique skills or knowledge that will be useful to reporters when a particular story breaks. Pediatricians at your hospital could be very useful in helping media understand child health issues in another country. Amateur historians can be a good resource in helping local reporters grapple with a subject. If one of your executives worked in Bosnia, and that country happens to be back in the news, then he or she may be of assistance to journalists, and at the same time reflect favorably on your organization.

- Understand that sometimes we market to the media and not the public. The press release may have limited public appeal yet it's in your best interest to make sure that media are notified of the event or accomplishment. Awards to your leadership fall into this category. Sometimes you want to reinforce the fact that you represent honorable people doing an honorable job regardless of its public merit.

- Acknowledge that the issue or item they are trying to promote will not work now, yet it may be successful later if you promote it during times when the media needs stories (like weekends). The summer months or the weeks immediately preceding or after major holidays such as Christmas or the Fourth of July may be prime times for advancing stories that would not work during busier times of the year.

- Acknowledge that timing is everything. A promotion that went nowhere is suddenly a big hit because of related national news. Always be ready to act on new events.

- Know that there are major differences between markets. What you cannot get in a major regional paper is a delight for the smaller publication. Market your opportunities where they will have the greatest effect. The "smaller" paper can still place your story on the Associated Press wire. You may get lucky with your "local" story and suddenly get regional placement.

- Understand that they can have considerable influence regarding a particular issue. The Fire Marshall in Maryland will demonstrate the burning of Christmas trees in different parts of the state to warn people that they need to exercise caution with lights and to water the tree frequently. They obtain tons of publicity because of the timely nature of the event, a dynamite visual plus a dose of news.

- Know that versatility can have a tremendous payoff. You may pitch a story to a television reporter yet it does not work because your proposed visual is less than compelling. Your willingness to return to your executives and brainstorm alternatives to an interesting photo opportunity may take a sow's ear and turn it into a silk purse.

- Approach their website (more on this later) as the perfect opportunity to market an organization. Regardless of your fellow bureaucrats who see the website as the perfect opportunity to place a long and boring overview of the history of widgets, you see your website in terms of its service and marketing potential.

- Are wizards in finding people to assist marketing efforts. Tom Sawyer would be envious of their ability to find helpful people. You discover that Fred in Accounting is a crackerjack amateur photographer. Sue in Accounts Receivable has a bachelor's degree in English and is a good writer. You find an electrician who once majored in advertising. It's not unusual to find all sorts of creative people looking to use their former or present talents in other ways.

- Establish a dollar figure for their proactive efforts. An advertising firm estimated that my Department of Public Safety efforts generated between two to four million dollars each year in proactive marketing. I never hesitated to advise my superiors about the amount produced to gain support for future projects.

Finally, you understand that the most important aspect of all your marketing efforts is to be seen as a willing participant in the public discussion of your organization and its issues. You're constantly "out there." Even in large and cumbersome markets, individual members of the media will notice your efforts. They hear you on the talk shows. They will see your media releases. They will be aware of your public affairs radio shows. They will see your organization on the 6 o'clock news.

They will read about your efforts in the local newspaper. They will come to understand that you and your organization are not afraid of larger public policy issues. They will admire you and your executives for your willingness to be part of the public debate. They will assume that if you're so willing to be so accessible, then you must be honorable people doing an honorable job. They will take this into account when your detractors come knocking. They will remember your efforts when you and the organization fall upon hard times.

The media has a way of coming to an understanding about who you and the organization truly are. You want to be seen as actively engaged and unafraid. This tactic will afford you a considerable amount of credibility that will protect you in the future.

Writing the Proactive Press Release

If you intend to announce a formula for turning rocks into gold, you do not need to offer anything more than a grammatically sound news release. The announcement of a cure for the common cold could be the most boring and lengthy news release in the world, but it will still work because of its subject matter. Writing the promotional release, however, takes a bit more ingenuity.

I was once told that are no rules to writing the promotional news release. I won't go that far but I do believe that considerable amounts of creativity and ingenuity are called for. You want to separate yourself from the mundane releases (ninety-eight percent of them) that go nowhere.

Spend a day in a television newsroom (yes, they will let you). Sit down with the young interns and lower-level employees who read incoming media releases. Ask them what attracts their attention, and prompts them to notify their assignment editors.

They will tell you that you have to establish your premise in the first two or three sentences. To do this, I use multiple headlines. I will use four and sometimes five headlines in large type to ensure that my point is made in the least amount of time. I know that my carefully crafted media release (that has been reviewed internally by everyone except the Pope) will live or die on the headlines. Whatever it takes, your appeal must have the ability to grab the media's attention and keep it.

Press release writing is an art unto itself. I submit to you that your headlines and first two paragraphs must communicate in such a way as to grab the person by the throat, throw him down to the floor and scream that your event or product is worthy of consideration.

If that involves three or four headlines of multicolored print in grammatically incorrect form that would embarrass your fourth grade English teacher, but forces the reader at the television station to pay attention, then you have successfully accomplished your objective. You have communicated.

Yes, I'm exaggerating, but not by much. We must be bold, creative, and sometimes just a little silly to get our point across.

The Rest of the Press Release

Per research, press releases with audio, video and photographs attached can get up to ten times the exposure compared to those without attachments. Tie your press release to your web and social media sites; offer video and audio. Beyond multiple and crystal clear (perhaps clever) headlines and the very judicious use of quotations from executives (exclude them if possible) the rest of the media release also needs attention.

The first consideration is that it should be as short as possible. Use large type (12 to 14 points) and short paragraphs. Brevity is next to godliness. Offer the basic elements of any issue or event. Describe the "who, what, when, where" elements of your story, devoting a sentence or two to each. Well-crafted releases describing who, what, when, and where plus a point of contact may be all you need. If you need descriptions of the product or policy you are trying to promote, then use very brief paragraphs. Your media release, under any circumstances, should be no longer than two pages. You should strive for a one-page media release.

The bottom-line issue is its interest to media and the larger public. Spell out your visuals. Give examples of the possibilities for sound that will entice radio stations. Describe your human-interest story in compelling terms. Tell readers how you will make it easy to cover your event. Tell them how the story connects with their readers, viewers, and listeners.

But there is a contradiction here. We have said that your mission is to make the reporter's job as effortless as possible. That is difficult to do in a one-page media release. There may be a wealth of materials (or other possibilities) that greatly add to the reporter's ability to do his or her job. If that's the case, then briefly advertise the availability of these materials and offer them to the reporter through e-mailed copies or by posting them on your website. Offer anything that works.

Note that many news organizations frown on e-mail attachments due to the possibility of malware. Put the material on your website and provide links.

Be sure to include your telephone number at the top or bottom of the release. Please remember to include after-hours numbers just in case they want to call you in the evenings or on the weekends. Your willingness to supply information off-hours can make a considerable difference as to whether your event is covered. Provide a cell phone number for the day of the event.

Distributing the Press Release

You need to have a comprehensive list of everyone in your market who could have influence. Segment the list by type of media. Obviously you need a list of media contacts, reporters, and assignment and future editors. But don't stop there. Include talk show hosts, bloggers, local newspapers and social media representatives. If they have an audience, market to them. I've known some who include religious leaders and their flocks in their distribution schemes.

There are a variety of surprisingly effective methods for distributing your news release. Simply e-mailing or faxing it to your intended audience is one of many options. Note that faxes are becoming obsolete and that some media have stopped taking them.

If you're trying to entice media, the best way is to e-mail the release to targeted reporters with personalized messages. Include a brief note telling them why this story is worthy of their interest. Include their names in the title and briefly describe the offer ("Hi, Tim. Dynamite visuals on Thursday," would be my pitch to the photo desk of a newspaper).

Phrases like "I have some great visuals to go along with the story," will be useful for television reporters. Or "this person is incredibly interesting," will be useful for a print journalist. To radio people, I emphasize great sound or the ability of a person to tell an interesting story.

Segment your lists. There is no sense in sending a geographic-specific release to the entire state or region. You may want options for bloggers, podcasters, assignment reporters, future desks, talk shows, morning news people, and others.

Ensure that your press release arrives no later than 5 a.m. Your notice must arrive in time for the morning broadcasts and decision meetings, often conducted at 8:00 or 9:00 a.m. Depending upon the importance of the event, I will send my notices several times to the same source. Often I will give them a week's notice. The second will go out two days before the event. A final notice will be sent the day of the event (marked "Today—Today—Today" at the top of the release). I will strive to offer something new, however small, in each media release. Yes, this is probably overkill, but overkill may be necessary when you are competing against so many.

As much as possible, call the newsroom and find out whether they have received the release. I have been told many times that they would have covered my event if they had known about it (yeah—I know—it's probably just an excuse). Just because you sent the release and confirmed that it went through does not mean that the right people are aware of it. As stated, newsrooms receive hundreds of requests every day. It is very easy for your release to get lost in the volume.

Calling key individuals (assignment or feature editors) and asking them if they are aware of your news release is a critical part of your strategy. You will find yourself resending the release to many. One way to avoid doing this is to not e-mail your release. When important enough, I will drive to select media and hand-carry the release to the right person. At times, I will also include a box of donuts with five or six media releases attached to the top. You may suggest that this is a bit hokey. You're right; it is. But I have found that a box of freshly baked donuts will get their attention every time.

Again, depending upon the importance of the situation, I will use Federal Express or Priority Mail. The bottom line is that I will do anything to make sure that my message is in the hands of the right person.

Not all Stories are Suitable for all Media

You have to decide the kind of story you are trying to promote. If you're advertising a new product, and you visit the factory where it's made, you may notice an environment that is rich in sound. Or the principal person responsible for your new achievement may have an easy-to-understand yet extremely interesting manner of speaking. These examples are radio stories.

One of the three prison systems in the state of Maryland is the Patuxent Institution. Out of a multitude of prisons built in the mid-1950s throughout the country that were designed to rehabilitate criminal offenders, the Patuxent Institution is the only one left. Under Maryland law, Patuxent is completely separate from the mainstream prison system and has its own authority to release and supervise inmates.

For many years, the person running this facility was an extraordinarily interesting professional who started his career as a psychiatric nurse.

He was from Ireland and continued to carry a considerable Irish brogue. People love to listen to this man. Needless to say, because of his interesting background and his melodious use of words, he was the perfect radio interview. Whenever we promoted his institution, radio was on our minds.

When I represented the state police, I thought of television. Nothing was more visually intriguing than a police car roaring down the street with lights flashing. The state police have all sorts of interesting visuals including mobile command centers, helicopters, bomb squads, and SWAT teams. Often the mere offer of placing a reporter and cameraperson inside of a police car was enough to carry the day.

Equally as obvious is the fact that some stories can best be told in print. Some issues are complicated to the point where you want the public exposed to easy-to-read descriptive statistics. Some individual stories are so compelling that they cannot be told in a minute's worth of television coverage.

A front-page newspaper photo can provide gripping evidence in support of the item or issue you're trying to promote. And as previously stated, the Associated Press or other services are more likely to pick up a newspaper story and spread it statewide or nationally.

Asking for Favors

Try your best never to ask media to cover a story as a favor. Although you are under tremendous pressure to advance the issue, it is rarely worth the trouble. Asking for consideration under these circumstances is no different from begging. This is beneath you and the organization. I will freely admit that I sometimes daze those within my organizations through aggressive promotions, but I will not beg for news coverage.

It's your job to offer compelling reasons to entice coverage. If it's not newsworthy, doesn't present a compelling visual, or lacks human interest, then don't promote it. I understand that this is easier said than done when executives want publicity. Many of us are under immense pressure to gain publicity for an endeavor deemed important by management. We're told that it is vital to the organization for the event to receive widespread publicity; but some of our executives have unrealistic ideas about what's promotable.

It's vital for you and your organization to be seen as honorable people. Public affairs professionals who ask for coverage of non-newsworthy items compromise that sense of honor. The other obvious difficulty of asking for favors is the fact that they will ask for something in return. The price paid to satisfy their request may be more than you are willing to pay.

Successful promotions are based upon a willingness to seek a newsworthy aspect of the story and its creative placement. It is up to you to find the right mix of elements to produce a successful promotion.

Branding

As stated, a brand could be a corporate logo, the company flag, unified website, company colors, a slogan or anything that reinforces the public's perception of who and what you are. There are endless books on branding, so the goal here is to establish some basic principles. Do you have an honest perception about who you are and what you do? I would submit that most have trouble answering this question.

Boil your organization's mission down to a sentence or two. I've seen bureaucracies take days of seclusion trying to establish basic principles. When done, everything you create should be supportive of these basic goals. A mission statement is part of this process, but mission statements are often endlessly wordy and confusing documents that few pay attention to. Brands need to be brief and clearly convey what you do. The question is, what conveys the message seamlessly? What's your slogan? What symbol conveys that message? What will you incorporate into everything you do?

Big corporations will be relentless about establishing a brand. Can you imagine Apple or Google without their corporate logos? Both immediately convey quality, innovation, and success.

Sit down with trusted advisors and establish a brand and logo. Test them with interested audiences. Go to Creative Commons for publically accessible artwork. Review stock photography. Work with volunteer artists. Ask a graduate marketing class at the local college or university for assistance.

Establishing a centralized brand can be useful to the well being of the overall organization. The same can be true for your marketing efforts.

You want to be seen as a concentric whole with one message and one brand because it's easier and much more effective to do it that way. Multiple messages within the same organization are confusing to the public and the media. They should be avoided.

Competing News Events

I once publicized an affair where the Governor was handing out awards to citizens and police officers engaged in anti-crime efforts. A lot of work went into publicizing the recipients and the event. We assumed that major media within the Washington/Baltimore market would not be as interested as those representing smaller communities where many of the individuals lived. We did everything possible to alert the smaller markets and community newspapers that had individuals from their area receiving this honor. We tried to develop as many human interest stories as possible with local angles. The great bulk of our coverage came from these efforts, but I was determined to try to bring major media into the main event when they received their awards from the Governor or Lieutenant Governor. I worked very hard to establish something interesting about an affair that many in the media saw as rather boring.

On the appointed day, I had promises from four television stations in two markets that they would attend my event based on compelling human interest stories. I did not expect anything more than 30 seconds on the evening news, but I would be very happy with that.

Approximately one half-hour before the event, a single engine plane crashed in the Chesapeake Bay approximately 10 miles away.

Needless to say, they abandoned my affair for this "newsworthy" and visual event.

All of us live with the disappointment of aggressive marketing of non-hard news items only to be superseded by the events of the day. It's an unfortunate reality that comes with the territory. Some of your executives will insist that you call the station and demand promised coverage. This attitude is naïve. The media will do what is in their best interest.

At 11:00 a.m., they felt your dog and pony show (or lunch) was preferable. At 11:30, it changed to a plane crash. There is nothing that any of us can do but smile and chalk it up to experience. Soft news will be superseded by hard news every day. It's something that we all need to learn to live with.

Write the Story Yourself

There are two primary rules of effective promotions: giving the media what they want and making it as easy as possible for them to cover you. Within the theme of making it easy, I would suggest that you write, video, or record your own news story. A lot of individuals are surprised to hear that you can do this. Not only can you write your own newspaper story; you can also write radio scripts within the confines of the article or a media release. You can create your own audio; you can create your own video.

There is an art to writing your own story. If you write it as any newspaper person would then, you have a much better chance of it being placed in the local newspaper under your own byline and organizational affiliation. If you write it to be a purely self-serving vehicle with endless quotes from your executives about a subject that is of little interest to anyone, then it's an exercise in futility.

If the article is a glowing account of your organization, it will be dismissed. It needs to be balanced, factual, and relevant. If you write it as straight copy that any newspaper person would enjoy reading then you have an opportunity for placement in local newspapers throughout your market. Major newspapers will not take it, but you did not expect that.

If you have 30 local newspapers within your market and 10 choose to run your article, or a segment of your article, then you have just reached tens of thousands of people with verbiage you control. If it's used as a letter to the editor it still serves the same purpose.

No one expects you to reach out to your detractors for comments, but thousands will read your point of view and be exposed to your communication objectives. Variations of the article can be submitted to trade publications. I do articles all the time for national professional publications and websites, and when printed, I place them on my website and advertise them through a press release.

At other times, reporters will take your article, interview you, and rework it as their own, which is fine as far as you're concerned. The self-written article is nothing more than a leveraged press release. As long as you are responsible in promoting your own interests and the article is newsworthy or interesting, you will do fine.

The same can hold true for video. There are colleges and community access stations that will film you or your agency heads (in studio) for a very reasonable fee. If you're willing to bring visuals or existing video, they will include footage of activities as you or your executives speak (known as "B- roll"). Sometimes they will create the footage for you and incorporate it into the program.

I have been hosting award-winning radio and television shows for over 20 years and I offered our products to radio and television stations throughout the market. It's a very successful form of promotion. Note that in many markets, spokespeople are creating their own video and audio and are creating nice products for very reasonable costs.

Marketing to Employees

All of us acknowledge the benefits of external marketing. Many of us, however, do not see the advantage of marketing to our own employees. Could such an effort have a payoff that would foster better internal relations as well as fewer instances of negative media?

In today's social media era, marketing to employees is more important than ever. In fact, there is research involving companies indicating that those with social media-involved employees who are supportive of the organization's message have significantly higher profits than those who do not.

A long time ago as a young police officer, I would gather with my brethren, have a drink or two, and cynically complain about those idiots at headquarters. Then I became an idiot at headquarters. After more than four decades of work, I have never forgotten the caustic remarks of those on the front lines. It would not surprise me to discover that the vast majority of employees of any organization are somewhat distrustful of the people occupying the upper rungs of management. Surveys of job satisfaction typically show that many of us are not terribly happy with our jobs.

They say that politics is a blood sport primarily because so many people win and lose with great frequency. The same can probably be said for corporate and government executives.

Employees at the lower levels often feel no allegiance to those at top. If they can cause them discomfort (or worse) by talking to reporters and releasing documents, they will. It is also not unusual for union representatives to suggest openly that employees contact the media if things do not go their way. So employees of any organization can cause either quite a bit of trouble or support. The question then is the efficacy of marketing to them.

First of all, you would hope that the organization pays and treats its employees well enough to forestall negative feelings. But my experience is that employees will continue to gripe regardless of their circumstances. Part of all of this is a subcultural reaction to their position within the organization.

Is there a way of addressing this built-in sense of discontent? Is there a way for the larger organization to make all or most employees feel that they're part of the team and share the same fate? Some companies have found a way to accomplish this. Apple and Google, for example, are world famous for their ability to engage their workforce in meaningful and productive ways. Their employees are known for their innovation and dedication to a common goal. The company also pays extremely well, with salaries and stock options designed to make all employees feel that they're benefiting from the success of the company. But entities like Apple and Google are rather rare.

So again we turn to the question of whether there is an effective way to market to most employees. In my opinion, this is one of the most difficult tasks that any organization can take on. But take it on we must.

Most employee newsletters are terrible. Most outreach efforts seem to be halfhearted. Much of the research focusing on employee satisfaction seems to deal with the inadequacy of front line supervisors. Many employees simply believe that they are not treated well by management. I have often wondered about the tremendous good that could occur if immediate supervision were trained in the art of good employee communications.

I am simply suggesting that there is room for improvement. We must be aggressive in our outreach efforts to employees at every level of the organization. Employees need to have some way of constructively expressing their feelings. They need to be responded to in meaningful ways. Employee communications need to address the primary concerns of staff.

Instead of these publications being designed by people at headquarters, I have often wondered what the results would be if we formed focus groups of employees and asked them how to improve internal communications, or what they would like to see in employee publications.

It's also time to get away from the word "publication." We now have audio and video at our disposal. Both should also be used.

I believe that every person in the executive branch should have a work phone at home with a recording device. The telephone number should be offered to employees. They should feel free to call and offer suggestions, complaints, and say whatever is on their mind. They should be able to do this anonymously, or to have the option of getting a telephone call back. E-mail can serve the same purpose.

None of this is to negate the issue of wages and benefits or the ability to gain as the organization profits. I also believe little gestures such as pens, hats, and coffee mugs or certificates or plaques of appreciation can go a long way in improving morale. Most surveys of job satisfaction indicate that employees need to feel appreciated. Show them that they are!

I believe that employees contact the media because they feel they have no other redress. That's sad.

I'm not suggesting decent treatment of employees solely as a tactic to improve external relations. All of us want decent treatment of everyone in the organization. I just wonder if all of those negative stories generated as a result of disgruntled employees could be lessened somewhat by a better mechanism of listening to their concerns and making them feel respected and listened to.

In the final analysis, I believe most organizations would probably conclude that it's easier and better for everyone involved to sit down with each other and talk.

E-Mail Is Vital

A bit more on e-mail. We embrace social media, promotional, and digital strategies and forget that the most powerful tool of all beyond paid advertising is e-mail. The research is clear—professional advertisers use traditional and digital paid media campaigns first, e-mail second, and social media third.

The development of a good e-mail list is vital to promoting your organization, and it's a great leveler with professional advertisers. They employ very sophisticated and costly e-mail platforms. We use Aweber (http://www.aweber.com) and MailChimp (http://mailchimp.com). Both are reasonably priced platforms that provide lots of instruction. At my federal and state agencies we used Outlook; it's cantankerous but you can make it work for hundreds of e-mail addresses. Regardless of the platform, maintaining an e-mail list is a little bit of hell. It constantly needs updating, maintenance, and of course, it needs to be populated with new addresses.

Regardless, people pay attention to e-mails if:

- They are relevant.

- You provide incentives.

- They use the person's name in the heading and first sentence.

- They offer something new, interesting, and service-oriented.

- They offer photos or links to video, audio, and other useful information.

- You send infrequently (no more than once a week unless you have a special promotion).

- You send in the morning. Note that for some consumers, weekend e-mail is best.

- They are segmented into usable categories. There's no sense in sending an e-mail to an area where the service or event does not apply.

- You limit attachments. Many systems will automatically reject any e-mail with an attachment. If you send a press release, please do not send as an attachment. Place the copy in the body of the e-mail.

- If you send a press release, send it no later than 5:00 a.m. to ensure it's there for morning decision meetings.

- You offer incentives to people who sign up for your e-mail list (e.g., a free e-book or a discount).

While I send blast e-mails all the time to everyone, it does not take a lot of time to do it manually. Create a standard e-mail and use this format to add a personal message to a reporter. Be sure to use the reporter's name in the heading of the e-mail (e.g., Hi, Mike. Great

Human Interest Stories Today). Let reporters know of the news value, human interest, or visual/sound quality opportunities available in the opening sentence.

Follow up with a phone call. It won't work without personal outreach.

Word-of-Mouth Promotions

We live in an age of social and traditional media and advertising, and we instinctively lean towards these activities when we think of promotions. That can be a big mistake. Sometimes we need to think in terms of established personal networks.

Research tells us that recommendations from friends and family is the most potent factor when it comes to U.S. consumers making purchasing decisions. Television ads are next in importance, followed by a recommendation from someone in your social circle. The next most effective category is an online review from someone you do not know in real life. Thus, a personal recommendation is more powerful than magazine, radio, social media, and billboard or newspaper ads.

Personal recommendations are the lifeblood of promotions. We invest tons of money and time into social media and traditional advertising, but often forget that our established networks can be far more powerful.

MyLifeAudio.com

I created a website devoted to telling personal life stories (http://mylifeaudio.com). I've done them with newspaper editors, historians, war veterans, high-ranking government officials, business people, individuals or sons or daughters who want their parents interviewed. With this site, I offer hosted audio or video recordings and place them on their own self-maintaining website along with photos and written material. I'm the host, and I ask questions, guiding guests through the interview process.

I created a nice website to promote the service and proceeded to write articles on the subject while promoting all through social media. I solicited user groups of like-minded people for advice and changed the site as necessary. When I got little to nothing in terms of search interest, I turned to Google AdWords. There was some improvement but not much.

I then paid a consultant who advised professional historians (a generic term for what I propose to do). She said the following:

"People are not searching for someone to tell their story through hosted interviews. What you are proposing is new and possibly brilliant and wanted, but it doesn't lend itself to being found through search."

"Ok," I said to myself, "I have millions of visitors and page views through previous digital efforts, and I just created something that has no relevancy to the search process? How dumb is that?"

"So what do I do?" I asked the consultant.

She told me that professional historians do best when it's through word of mouth. Ask clients to recommend you. Ask your friends, family, and professional contacts to promote your site. Do the same on social media. Speak to groups about what you do and how you plan to do it.

Some of my Web efforts work beautifully and some don't. The lesson is that there is no fixed strategy to promotions; you have to seek your market through trial and error.

Those Interested

We tend to forget that one of your most powerful promotional platforms are friends, family, business associates, and those interested in what you do. Create flyers, articles, audio and video, and send links through e-mail and social media. Ask recipients to spread the word. Encourage their audiences to repost. If they like what I'm trying to do and ask others to spread the message, then it has the potential for reaching lots of people.

There is research indicating that opinions of strangers via digital media are as believable as personal recommendations from friends. It's the new word-of-mouth advertising. Salespeople advocate networking all the time. Please consider.

CHAPTER EIGHT: MEDIA YOU CONTROL: WEBSITES, PODCASTS AND SOCIAL MEDIA

I want to share my experiences with websites, social media, and related platforms because it dramatically changes our relationship with the public and media. For decades, I was beholden to reporters to reach the public. That is no more. We can now say what we want in the way we want through websites, self-produced audio and video, and social media.

We now have partial control of our reputations. I do not see much of a distinction between websites, podcasts, and social media. All are platforms to post content to and are used to interact with visitors. I can build a really nice website and create great content, but have minimal views and engagement. I can repost the same subject matter on social media and engage in hundreds of conversations. We need to figure out the formula for ourselves.

Why do all this? It accomplishes organizational objectives. It advances the goals of the agency. It protects the organization. It serves customers. My content creation and social media efforts have paved the way for positive media reports and customer interactions. They explain complicated topics and turn detractors into supporters. Major agency initiatives are successful because of the exposure.

We had a project where we tried to convince criminal offenders with warrants to surrender voluntarily. We did audio interviews with two participating (the first in line to surrender over two days) and immediately placed them on our audio podcasting site backed by a press release and social media. Both told fascinating stories as to why they choose to participate. Media immediately responded to compelling storytelling; we gained multiple television and radio interviews that convinced others to participate. We went from uncertainty to success in a matter of hours. Thus the power of content creation and social media serves organizational interests and provides new tools for success.

Note that I have personal and professional sites, and I help others develop a digital presence. My observations will come from all three experiences.

There are endless digital platforms and no one can keep up with them all. I just posted an article on my Facebook page (https://www.facebook.com/leonardsipes) reporting that Snapchat is used by seventy-seven percent of college students every day. But I have no intention to use the service unless I represent or talk to collegiate institutions.

As to background, I suggest listening to tech podcasts (specifically "This Week in Tech") and subscribing to Marketing Charts and Search Engine Land (see http://leonardsipes.com for links), but the digital world is fast-paced and forever chaining.

I will make some suggestions about platforms, products, and software based on information and data available today, but I have no idea what their relevance will be five years later. Facebook may dominate now, but Facebook can collapse in a heartbeat if something new and better comes along (remember America on Line?).

Finally, there are endless numbers of books, DVDs, podcasts, and websites providing instructions and guidance on websites, social media, and the creation of audio, video, story-based articles, and other materials. Again, see the "Best Resources for Media and Social Media" article at http://leonardsipes.com for recommended resources.

I'll refer to podcasting throughout the rest of this chapter. Podcasting is creating a series of audio and video programs and placing them on the Internet. It's not my intention to recreate the endless thousands of pages of existing material on digital platforms or to provide hands-on instruction on how to create video or audio. What follows are my experiences and lessons learned.

Digital Credentials

Many claim to be social media experts, thus everyone justifiably asks for credentials and experience. I've created or participated in the creation of a wide variety of professional and personal websites. It's the same for social media platforms. I've helped develop them for government, associations, nonprofits, and a couple of businesses. I travelled the country speaking at conferences about developing a social media and public relations presence. I've met with agency heads and senior staff from a wide variety of major government agencies and associations to advise them on a social media policy and operations. People pay me considerable sums of money for a couple hours of instruction.

I have about twenty years of experience hosting radio and television shows and approximately 15 years of posting those shows on the Internet (podcasting). I create my own radio shows, and I'm in the process of learning video and green screen production. I was the first state agency on the Internet with a radio and television series and the first federal agency to do the same. I have a long history of interacting with digital users (my definition of social media). I have lots of national and regional awards for my digital work.

What's essential is an understanding of how digital media interacts with and affects media and public relations. What's even more important is that you realize that your principle role will be that of writer and content creator. No one is asking you to be a technical expert.

Not a Technocrat

Millions are creating websites without an ounce of coding experience, principally through WordPress, Squarespace, and Blogger. There are billions of YouTube videos created by 14-year-olds.

Your smartphone and tablet are both a more than adequate source of audio, video, and photographs. There are editing platforms that require no prior knowledge of video or audio. There are endless, user-friendly do-it-yourself videos through Mac University, YouTube, and Linda.com (among others) that provide instruction.

You do not have to have specific technical knowledge to do anything I'm proposing. The real tech-savvy people who taught me exist within your organization and local colleges. Seek them out. You can do this. It's exciting and creative. It unleashes your inner desire to express yourself and your organization's message. If you feel a bit intimidated, join the crowd; you're not alone. If I can do this, you can do this.

Somewhat Informal

Please understand that Web-based material is meant to be somewhat informal. My radio shows are done in one take; I have no aspirations to emulate National Public Radio. Mistakes are left in; it simply seems more friendly and real that way.

My television shows use the same philosophy; I'm not there to compete with 60 Minutes. My shows are not heavily scripted. Articles and podcasts do not have to be long. A four-paragraph update or a two-page overview is peachy. Sometimes a two-minute video or audio is all you want or need. We need to rid ourselves of the notion of extremely high production values. It impedes creation and good communication.

There are simple tools that create very acceptable programs. We have to pay attention to audio quality (sixty percent of good video is good audio) but that's remedied by using wired lapel microphones. Paying lots of attention to microphone levels and testing the sound before you record almost eliminates the need for editing audio after recording.

Be real, be entertaining, be friendly, inform, and offer a service. Be the very opposite of government or corporate-produced media. Use photographs and supporting footage in your videos. Respect learning styles by offering a variety of media. Remember that some like to listen while others like to view a video or read a fact sheet or a story-based article.

Interchangeable

Much of what I write is interchangeable and applies equally to Web and social media sites and podcasting. Addressing websites and social media separately helps me frame the discussion a bit, but 95 percent of lessons apply to both. To me, a Facebook organizational page "is" a website. The same applies to Twitter, LinkedIn, Google Plus or any other social site. All need to be designed and populated with care. Getting artwork is essential, especially for the banner.

Push to the Website

I've been to a variety of national and regional digital, blogging, and social media conferences and meet-ups where the goal was to get people to your website through social media. This now seems dysfunctional; people are reluctant to leave social media sites unless there is a very good reason. Social platforms are distinct places where people come to read, view, listen, interact, and have fun.

Social sites have their own personalities and pretty much stand on their own. My material is routinely ignored on one and endlessly debated on another.

Thus, we may want to think of the digital world as multiple platforms that you need to maintain, populate, and interact with. A friend refers to this as "feeding the beast." It never ends, and it never slows down; please keep this in mind as you develop a digital strategy. Only develop what you are willing to maintain.

Note that some are claiming that Facebook is getting them

considerable traffic for their websites, but's that's based on paid promotions. If you have the budget to pay for traffic via Facebook ads, it's something that you may want to pay attention to.

Every Day?

Do I go to my Twitter page every day? Nope, I simply don't have the time to pay strict attention to all my social platforms. Organizations with money can hire companies to do it for them or use free or paid software that analyzes transactions. I use e-mail (that alerts you to comments on your sites) and Google Alerts to keep track of what's happening in the social world. Larger organizations and social "experts" will express astonishment that I do not use available free and paid tools, but I have to talk to reporters, write documents, do promotions, go to meetings, and everything else that comes with the job. It's not perfect, but it will have to do.

Responding

The very essence of websites and social media is that it's supposed to be social, thus an interaction. That means when people write, I respond. I do make an attempt to reply meaningfully to every comment.

I spent weeks advising a major federal agency on social media and audio and video podcasting, and they decided to use Facebook and other services. They would "allow" comments, but they had no intention of responding to them. While it was a step in the right direction, it remains a silly decision.

Discussions within social platforms can be meaningful. First, it provides direct contact with a vast bureaucracy. Second, you build good relations. Third and most important, you get valuable feedback about your agency or corporation. People tell you what you're doing right and what you need to do a better job.

Via social media, someone advised us that there was a flaw in the technology we used to keep track of offenders. He was right. We had a phone conversation and then I arranged for a discussion with our experts.

Many of us use social media principally as a broadcast network to get the word out about a new product or service, and that's fine. But if you choose not to interact meaningfully, it seems to me that social media is a disingenuous act that reinforces your organization's reputation as less than honorable.

Rarely Overwhelming

Responding to social media generated questions and comments is manageable. I have fact sheets and a ton of prepared material that answers most questions. When appropriate, I will respond personally.

My Web and social media sites are rarely overwhelming. I understand that many don't create a social presence, or use it improperly based on the perception of the work it requires (that and the fear of saying something wrong), but it's manageable.

The exception is reacting during difficult times. When you're down, everybody wants to pile on. It's impossible to respond to thousands of messages calling you and your organization scumbags. Thank them for their comments and tell them that you take their observations seriously. Put them into categories and make sure that leadership is aware of the messages and numbers.

You need to develop a system of fresh content that meets user needs. The heart and soul of a digital presence is content creation. I find that weekly 30-minute radio programs are relatively easy to create, and people seem to like them. It's the same with my 30-minute television programs. I probably create about fifty to sixty new products a year, including original and updated documents for my federal site and that's enough to keep the conversation going. I like to release something new on a weekly basis.

Reposting on Social

I repost material from my websites on Facebook, Twitter, LinkedIn, Reddit, Google Plus, and Tumblr, StumbleUpon, YouTube, and Digg. There are endless others I do not use. Others (Blog Catalog, Alltop, Facebook's Networked Blogs) automatically repost on their sites when I place an article on mine.

My current project is marketing to groups within Facebook, Google, LinkedIn and Reddit. It seems to be working. When I analyze traffic for my personal and professional sites, I find that different social sites will take the lead in referring traffic to my website. This is not unexpected. Social sites have different audiences and varied demographics. What works for one topic does not work for all. But really, considering it's so easy to repost content to a social media site, why not include the largest and most influential regardless of demographics?

I try to repost material on social sites in the mornings on workdays; research seems to support this strategy. I will post a similar message on Twitter several times.

Facebook is by far the most popular social media site; time spent is remarkable. Where most websites record very short times on a page, Facebook is the clear exception. Organizations create "Pages" and individual users use "Profiles." There is considerable disagreement about which one (Pages or Profiles) organizations should use. Facebook Page posts are sent only to a small fraction of users without paid advertising, and not everyone sees your Profile entries.

Facebook wants you to pay them to distribute your material to everyone and for some; they claim considerable success through advertising. Thus, Facebook may be the world's biggest social platform, but it has considerable limits without the ability or willingness to pay money to advertise.

Hashtags (#) allow for the searching of similar terms and phrases through Twitter. Facebook and Google Plus have similar capabilities. Hashtags allow us to market to people searching for a term or phrase and it helps us keep track of what people are saying about us, or the topics we're interested in.

Just remember that except for new websites, search engines will send the majority of traffic, and then e-mail with social media being last. E-mail, however, will give you the highest rate of conversion (people taking action).

Reposting Via RSS

Now this is exciting: RSS stands for "Really Simple Syndication." It means that organizations automatically add your offerings to their websites. Universities and major organizations throughout the world place my radio and television shows on their own sites. It happens automatically. I do not have to lift a finger. They find your RSS feed and add it to their sites. Internet television and radio also use my federal programs via RSS. The RSS feed for my personal website is http://www.leonardsipes.com/feed/.

Note that most understand RSS as a platform to send new material to individual readers, and as I write this book, this seems to be diminishing rapidly.

Do I Understand Websites and Social?

I used to think that I knew a lot about websites and social media; we were one of the first state and federal agencies to use it (yes, I got in early) and I rank incredibly well in Google and Bing and had millions of page views on my work-related websites (per server statistics). I supported my website activities by reposting content on Facebook, Twitter, LinkedIn, and other platforms.

At a conference where I was speaking, someone caustically asked me if I ever started a non-government Web and social site from scratch?

"Nope," I answered.

"Then, sir, you don't know social," he firmly stated. "You're a 'dot gov,' and that's how you get all those page views and great rankings for your website. Google likes you because they presume authority. You represent a federal agency, so you immediately get Facebook followers. Try creating a non-federal website and social media presence from scratch and then come back and tell me your lessons learned," he said with a sneer.

Since then I started several websites of my own, all backed by Facebook, Twitter, and other social platforms, and have helped others with their government, nonprofit, and association sites. I took his challenge and quickly found that he was right. You do not know website development and social platforms until you fight, scratch, and claw for every page view.

Some organizations are going to get followers immediately and people willing to interact. They usually represent companies and individuals backed by millions of dollars of advertising and traditional media. There are hundreds of thousands of people who love cola drinks who will follow Pepsi to the grave. Why I do not know, but they do.

There are brands and sites that quickly attract millions of followers without much effort. If you build Jeep Wranglers or motorcycles, or you are a national religious or political leader, or popular musician, build it and they will come.

What I want everyone to understand is that their experience may not be yours. Social media and websites are not and cannot be cookie-cutter recipes for communications. An article in Search Engine Land claims that ninety-five percent of all websites get fewer than 30 unique visitors a day. What I do for my federal sites is essentially what I do for my personal sites and the differences in traffic are remarkable. Note that one personal site (http://crimeinamerica.net), however, does better than my federal websites because it fills a niche.

Nothing is so humbling than creating a digital presence. Just keep in mind that there are many ways to communicate and promote, digital is just one. It offers no guarantees.

The Social Media Revolution

Social media provides you with a free (relatively speaking) platform to interact with thousands or millions of people. You have tools for direct communication. It may be the most revolutionary form of communication since the invention of radio or television.

The Pew Research Center's Internet Project in 2014 states that "73% of online adults now use a social networking site of some kind. Facebook is the dominant social networking platform in the number of users, but a striking number of users are now diversifying onto other platforms. Some 42% of online adults now use multiple social networking sites." As tantalizing as those numbers sound, most of us are able to reach only a small fraction.

We've already addressed my definition of social media as an all-encompassing integration of websites, social media sites, podcasts, and other platforms. It's digital or Internet communication that invites users to respond or repost. The heart and soul of social media is content creation through story-based efforts. Social media works only when you create interesting subject matter and people interact and share.

To most it's Facebook, Twitter, Google+, LinkedIn, YouTube, Instagram, and an endless number of places where people post comments, video, and photos and interact. Understand that the use of the term is evolving, and we are learning more with each passing day. All of us are trying to figure social out. All we are truly sure of is that it's growing and becoming more influential every day. Social is not the principal driver of website traffic or a primary mechanism to get people to do things now. But many see it as a growing and powerful platform for the future.

Why Do Social?

Why do social? There are endless reasons:

- You have the opportunity to influence thousands or millions of people.

- Your organization can be destroyed (OK, significantly hampered) by social media. You have to be involved. You have to understand how it works. If for no other reason beyond the potential for danger, you should become proficient in social media.

- For many organizations without an advertising budget, social media, e-mail, and your website may be your only options to communicate and influence.

- It allows you to respond quickly to emerging issues. It's a key tool during emergencies and tough times. If you do it right, media will appreciate your efforts.

- Your website and social media platform works 24/7/365 to represent your organization. Regardless of the time and day, you have an electronic spokesperson providing accurate information.

The Research

Few have a good idea about what we mean by social media and its effectiveness. The following is a very short summation of recent research. Although the research cited pertains to business, I believe the lessons are transferable to all organizations. Most data comes from Marketing Charts (http://www.marketingcharts.com/), Search Engine Land (http://searchengineland.com/) and my own observations documented through my professional and personal websites. I post most sources for my observations below on my Facebook page at https://www.facebook.com/LeonardSipes.

Taking Action

It's uncertain what having thousands of social media followers really means from a communications perspective. There is strong evidence that social is great for branding or raising awareness, but left unanswered is whether people are taking specific actions (like buying something) as a result of social media. This conclusion is supported by multiple research sources.

Do We Respond?

Research indicates that many of the organizations contacted via social don't respond to the majority of messages and comments (although the percentages are getting better). When they do come, it's not necessarily a meaningful experience for the customer. Thus, the very essence of what we understand as social seems questionable.

Raving Fans?

Will you create a community of raving fans? Unless you are a corporation or entity backed by millions of dollars of advertising or someone famous, probably not. What you will do, however, is create an opportunity for thousands of people to be exposed to your message in new and unique ways.

By the way, the term "Raving Fans" is used endlessly on the Web and in social literature to describe people who are brand enthusiasts with regard to products or services. If a Search Engine Land article is correct and the vast majority of websites get 30 unique visitors or fewer every day, your odds of getting those fans are bleak.

Interaction

Thousands will interact with what we do, correct? Probably not.

I ran national clearinghouses (both connected to the nation's most successful public service advertising campaign backed up by tens-of-millions of dollars of television and radio ads) and few called or wrote for additional information or offered comments or criticisms (this was pre-Internet). Prepared fact sheets and prearranged material handled the vast majority of interactions.

Like the experience above, I created millions of page views for a variety of websites, but the comments and interactions were few. Most simply acknowledge and compliment. Again, prepared fact sheets handle most of the rest. I do, however, respond to every unique inquiry.

The premise that social media is a platform for the exchange of views or the resolution of issues remains an open question. It works for me on my federal and state sites, but the response is hardly overwhelming. The only issue not in question is when bad news goes viral through social. "Participation" then takes on a brand new meaning. Finding yourself on the receiving end of hundreds or thousands of negative reviews is a nightmare.

The Quality Web

What's the principal thing to understand about social media? Those in business will tell you that 80 percent of purchases are made by 20 percent of customers. You have to influence the 20 percent.

This is what I call the "Quality Web." You do not have to influence everybody. You have to favorably affect those important to you. Your numbers could stink for your nonprofit but if several users give you tens of thousands of dollars because of your digital efforts, then you have succeeded. I understand that people want numbers, but if I influence partner agencies or Congressional aides or media through my work, then my efforts are successes.

Website Issues

It's a bit silly to discuss creating websites. Your organization undoubtedly has one. All I'm asking you to do it to make it better. There are organizations with terrible websites or those who exist solely on Facebook (bad idea).

Don't have a website? Want to improve yours? There are platforms like WordPress and SquareSpace and Google's Blogger that allow website development without an ounce of experience. My personal sites use WordPress. There are rather inexpensive "themes" and "skins" that go over the websites that you build (I use a specialist for the installation) that give your website the look and feel of a professionally developed site. You can develop a rather nice looking and very functional website for approximately $500.00, including labor.

Also note that the cost of entry into the web and social media world has dropped dramatically. You can create a video- and audio-based website and use social media for a tiny fraction of the expense it was ten years ago. What I spent for bandwidth years ago to host my radio and television shows ($25,000 a year) is now $10.00 a month on a shared server.

One can manage a website without knowing the mechanics. For larger organizations, website specialists need to be on board or be accessible. They are the ones who must ensure that our pages load in a reasonable amount of time and that our site is "manageable" for the majority of browsers and mobile platforms. There are times when I get stuck on my sites where I would rather spend some money to hire someone to fix things quickly than take hours trying to resolve the problem myself.

One word of warning—pay a service to back up your site. It's an expenditure you won't regret. It's a great comfort knowing that if you do something silly or get hacked you can always quickly rebuild.

Populating the Site

Writing for the Web is different than what you were taught in school. Everything we need to know is contained in documents on promotional writing and presentations. Let others worry about coding. I am solely concerned about the appearance of the site and the usefulness of its materials.

The operative word is "communicate." When people come to a website they must immediately feel welcome. If they do not establish a quick comfort level then they may (and probably will) abandon it for another.

Your site must be optimized for mobile devices (the future of the Internet). Just understand that there are still lots of users (in big cities and rural areas) that have limited bandwidth. I live in central Maryland and get blazingly hot wired Internet service "but" I have to leave my condo and go outside just to get access to my work-related cell service. My wireless experience on trains when I commute to D.C. is a disaster. Do not assume that all users have quick access to anything. Keep your sites light and responsive.

Websites should work flawlessly on Internet Explorer, Chrome, Firefox, Safari and all others. Photographs are essential. Work photographs into every article. There are plenty of stock photo sites available where the right to use quality photos, videos, or graphics is reasonable. Everything needs to be clean and crisp. The middle school student should feel at home. Everything needs to be easy to find.

Major issues or items that the organization wants to promote (or respond to) should be very easy to find, principally through highlighted boxes on the main page.

Every site should have a very easy-to-use search function. Colors and graphics should be easily downloadable. There should be lots of white space and little crowding. Pages should use plain language that the general public can easily understand.

Servers (even shared servers) are now at sufficient capacity to offer streaming audio and video with the right software, and you should take advantage of these possibilities. There are some users who rebel against reading a complicated position paper but will listen to audio or watch video presentations.

Ninety percent of your public inquiries should be answerable through your website. Every effort should be made to establish frequently asked questions. Every one of these questions should be within its own category.

Relevant, updated and easy-to-read publications should be offered for every question. It's perfectly fine and maybe even preferable to offer one-page fact sheets instead of longer documents. Short story-based articles (the kind that the media creates) should be a vital part of your content strategy. The heart and soul of digital media is content creation based on telling compelling stories. The primary difficulty of managing a website has nothing to do with the mechanics. The biggest problem is keeping materials relevant and fresh.

Managing your website becomes a dual responsibility. Specialists should be in charge of making sure that you have the right technology in the proper amounts and competent personnel to support your efforts. Others should manage your offerings and interact with a group of full-time or contractual writers or video and audio specialists.

Unfortunately, I've found many sizeable organizations with one webmaster (for the technical stuff) and one content manager for everything else. Unless supplemented by others, a two-person team is usually unable to create and manage a first-rate website.

Design Websites for the Average Person

Leaving your website solely in hands of technocrats is a sure recipe for problems. Technocrats see the world differently than the average person. Most of us want simplicity, relevancy and ease of use. Some technocrats love the complexity of technology. Ease of use may not be their principal goal.

Your content manager should have a good feeling for basic public affairs. Writers should keep the site constantly updated with fresh and easy-to-read materials. You should seek out individuals who know nothing at all about your subject matter to log on to your website and establish its relevancy. These individuals should be invited to a focus group and have their findings documented and circulated to the right people.

These points have little relevancy if you're running a site devoted solely to technical experts. If you're targeting lawyers, then feel free to pack it with long, inane, and complicated court decisions. They will be in hog heaven. But I strongly suggest that the vast majority of organizational websites be designed for the average person.

USA Today revolutionized the newspaper business through short articles. You may still feel more comfortable with The New York Times or The Wall Street Journal, but that does not change the fact that the face of communications is changing rapidly. If you choose to emulate USA Today as your boilerplate, you will do just fine.

Yours will be a popular source for easy-to-read materials that will reflect favorably on your public image. Users will see a courtesy and feel good about it.

Some Cautions

At the same time, it would be the height of hypocrisy to suggest that all of the documents on my professional websites were as easy to read as I would have liked them to be. Sometimes a technical document is the most complete and factual publication I have that answers a specific question. I do not have the time to rewrite hundreds of technical materials.

Much of what I have suggested above is the ideal and not necessarily a practical reality. It takes time and money to manage a major website plus related social media sites.

As I said earlier, anything can backfire. A digital presence only works if it's there to serve users in meaningful ways. Be harsh, deceptive, or unresponsive, and it can come crashing down on you in a second. I try to use the same tactics with all my sites and those I assist. Some work and some don't. Some get traffic and some stink.

Some topics lend themselves to a digital presence and some don't. If you're competing against thousands of websites that got there ten years ago, you have a real challenge on your hands. If you create a topic that few search for (like my previous reference to audio and video recordings via http://mylifeaudio.com) it's going to be a disappointing experience.

Some websites thrive through very traditional means like e-mail advertising or word-of-mouth campaigns, but their ability to get search engines to like them or have social media sites refer traffic to them can be very challenging.

Some websites work as a landing page for paid advertising. Some succeed because they invest in a "service to the media" strategy. In return for services rendered (i.e., opinions, research, quotes) media cites the website address in reports that reach hundreds of thousands who go to the website for additional information. That will be my strategy for http://crimeinamerica.net.

I believe in the principles I've stated here. I do believe in digital strategies and that we're rapidly moving towards the day when public affairs professionals (rather than tech people) will run websites, and content creation will take center stage.

Search Engine Optimization

Search engine optimization or SEO is endlessly debated in website circles. There are SEO experts who will spend thousands of hours analyzing your competition and your site.

They will suggest linking strategies. Links happen when other websites include your site or the address (URL) of your article or product on theirs. Search engines such as Google see links (especially from similar high-quality organizations) as indicators that your site is worthy of a lofty ranking in search results. The research seems clear. Most people do not go beyond the first five entries in a search, and some suggest they do not go beyond the first two or three.

There are endless strategies that prompt search engines to rank your site well, and I have no intention on offering a comprehensive review. Many (most?) have been discredited or discouraged. Moves by Google and other search engines to fight spam and unscrupulous links have left the SEO industry in disarray.

What Works?

- Create great content and people will link to your site (per Google).

- Serve user needs, not the organization's needs.

- Use keywords appropriately; if your site addresses the best way to use widgets in the creation of automobiles, then use "widgets" and "automobiles" in your title and first sentence so search engines and people can find you.

- Do not stuff your article with keywords.

- Communicate through a variety of media such as video, audio, story-based articles and fact sheets. Respect user preferences. There are an endless number of websites that feature photographs. Photography seems to be a powerful method of communication; it's something that you need to consider.

- Publish as often as you can. It may be nothing more than a photograph or a three-paragraph update. Post your material on YouTube and a variety of social sites.

- Promote through e-mail and work your website into your advertising.

- Develop a Google+ account. Link all of your Web and social sites to your account.

- Remember that people are overloaded with Internet options. They skim, they do not read. Get to the point.

- Mobile is the future of all things digital. Create for mobile platforms.

- Be prepared to work hard—very hard. Results can take years, not months.

What Really Works?

- Solve people's problems.

- Develop a site with little to no competition.

- Make people laugh.

- Reach an audience that appreciates what you do.

- Use pornography (I'm not serious but you need to know that many consider the real innovators of the digital word to be the porn industry).

- Stir strong emotions. Emotions are the central ingredient in getting something to go viral (be popular).

- Become famous.

- Spend millions of dollars advertising your site (again, I'm kidding but that's how new ventures and corporations do it).

Measuring Traffic

I was completely and utterly amazed by how many visits we got on my state and federal sites. Because we placed items of interest on our sites, we had tens-of-thousands of visitors a week for one year to well over 1.4 million page views a year for another. My Web-based radio and television shows seem to be well received.

But keep in mind that numbers are deceiving. A person can spend 30 minutes on Facebook (the clear leader as to time spent) or time watching the streaming version of the CBS Evening News or reading the Washington Post, but they often spend seconds scanning your web or social site. Time on site is rather small for most websites. Don't be shocked by your "time on site" numbers. Keep in mind that measurement of mainstream media, Web, and social use is hotly contested. There are endless ways to measure traffic and time on site. Few agree on what is meant by a visitor, page view, or a hit.

People trust Google Analytics but even Google does not measure everything. I use server statistics and exclude robot searches from search engines and other sources, but they are uniformly different (much more) than what I get from Google Analytics or WordPress. Also note that there are articles claiming that the majority of Web traffic comes from non-human sources (i.e., search robots). Just keep in mind that measurements of traffic can vary greatly from one source to another. As stated, I choose to use server statistics that identify and exclude robot searches.

But I'm convinced that the Internet and good content has the potential for being the primary method (beyond a paid advertising campaign, e-mail and personal recommendations) of positive public relations for many organizations. Anyone who does not use their Web and social sites as promotional tools is gravely in error. If I did nothing else throughout the year besides work on my web and social sites, then the efforts would probably be worth it.

Effective Communication?

There are endless communication options ranging from traditional old-school ads on radio, television, and newspapers to websites and e-mail. If you take a look at communication budgets from people who measure results (the professional advertising community), the overwhelming percent of ad campaign budgets continue to flow to strategies that the characters in Mad Men would embrace. Some sources state that social media currently constitutes no more than a small percent of most marketing budgets. Traditional advertising continues to rule. It's changing to greater investment in social, but it will take time for social to flourish fully.

Do not be fooled into thinking that a digital strategy will solve your communication problems. It's a tool, one strategy among many. Social media is not the best tactic for getting people to "do" things. Social is best for branding, raising awareness and for quickly getting the word out or respond to problems.

Social Media Has Issues

Even at a personal level, social media has issues. About one in two believe that social networking has no positive effect on how individuals interact with each other in society. A surprisingly large number also believe that social networking has not helped them strengthen relationships with family and friends. But possibly the most convincing piece of recent research is directed to those masters of all things digital—teenagers. American teens don't fancy everything digital when it comes to advertising. They strongly favor offline over online ads across a variety of measures.

Researching Companies

Most Americans try to proactively learn more about the companies they hear about or do business with. Social media and websites play a big part in that research.

So All This Means

We know that more than 70 percent of Internet users are engaging social media platforms, thus we feel compelled to engage them back through content creation.

There are doubts that social media prompts people to take desired actions.

Yes, social is great for raising awareness, but additional research on marketing states that most advertising still goes to traditional sources (television, radio and newspapers) thus reinforcing the belief that social is not a bedrock method of obtaining purchase or commitment decisions.

We know that more people use the Internet and social media to research everyone and there are high quality users who are important to your business or cause; you must appeal to them.

It's been my experience that the "quality Web" is the heart and soul of social media. These are users who are important to your bottom line. They pay attention and give time to digest what you create. This concept reinforces the old business adage that 20 percent of your customers are responsible for 80 percent of your sales.

Thus social media may be a game of massive numbers, but it's that 10 to 20 percent who propel your business or cause to success.

Afterword/Contact

It has been a pleasure sharing my thoughts and experiences with you, and I look forward to your comments. All of us learn from each other about how to become better at public relations and communications. Please do not hesitate to contact me if you have thoughts or criticisms.

If you enjoyed reading this book, please be sure to leave a review so that others working in and aspiring to careers in public affairs will be able to find it as well.

Please share your comments with others.

Connect with Leonard

As stated throughout this book, I offer media relations services, consulting, public speaking, social media, family histories and recorded audio and video interviews (podcasting). Contact me at leonardsipes@gmail.com or call toll free at 410-575-3127. Sign up for my newsletters at http://leonardsipes.com , http://mylifeaudio.com and http://crimeinamerica.net for updates on these and other services plus gain access to periodic discounts and programs that I make available only to subscribers.

I look forward to talking with you.

Bibliography-Quotations

Abraham Lincoln Online
(www.showcase.netins.net/web/creative/lincoln/html)

Bartlett's Quotations, (www.bartleby.com)

"Public and Media Relations" from the National Institute of Corrections at http://nicic.gov/Library/022948

Selected Quotations from Thomas Jefferson (www.monticello.org)

Made in the USA
Coppell, TX
30 June 2020